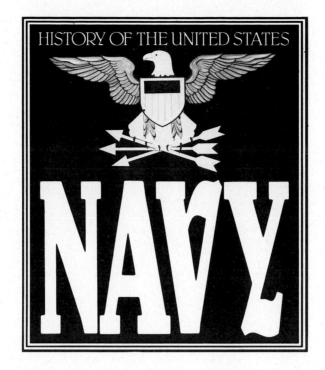

HISTORY OF THE UNITED STATES

NAVY

HISTORY OF THE UNITED STATES

NAVY

cp

ISBN 1 85361 061 5

Printed in Italy

CONTENTS

1: BIRTH OF A NAVY 1775-1798

When a new or reconstituted nation decides that its security and prosperity depends on maintaining an ocean-going navy, the results are liable to be as far-reaching as the oceans themselves. Over the past 120 years, culminating in the two World Wars of the 20th Century, this has certainly been the case with the new navies of Italy, Germany, and Japan. Remembering their influence on the Second World War alone, the creation of an ocean-going Soviet Navy since 1945 has been a most ominous accompaniment to the rapid decline, after centuries of paramountcy, of British sea power, the world's strongest until postwar relinquishment of Empire.

The mantle of global naval supremacy passed from the British to the United States Navy 40 years ago, in the latter years of the Second World War; and fortunately for the Free World the United States Navy remains the world's strongest in the 1980s. But the origins of American sea power present a startling contrast to the 'instant navies' so eagerly created by Italy, Germany, and Japan in their demand for recognition as world powers. Far from being an aggressive or nationalist demand for a 'place in the sun,' the creation of the United States Navy in the last decade of the 18th Century was a grudging, reluctant acceptance of unwelcome necessity. And this is all the more surprising because the United States only emerged as a new nation after successfully defying the most renowned naval supremacy since the Roman Republic defeated Carthage.

When resistance to the force of British arms began in the American 'Thirteen Colonies' in the spring of 1775, only a minority of American activists really believed that total independence from British rule was their true goal. There was little to indicate that 200 years later the colonists' descendants would be citizens of the world's most powerful nation, possessed of the strongest armed forces on the planet. Indeed, in 1775 this was virtually the status of Britain, whose control the American colonists felt driven to challenge. Only 12 years earlier, Britain had emerged as the victor in the first true world war: the Seven Years War (1756–63), which had seen France and her allies confounded in land and sea battles from Canada to Bengal. As British subjects, the American colonists had played their part in that victory, on land against the French and their surrogate Indian 'troops' in Canada, and at sea as privateers preying on French trade. The Colonies had also supplied some

18,000 seamen to the Royal Navy. In its origins, the War of American Independence should be seen as a violent series of strikes by the colonists against what they saw as arbitrary and unfair taxation to pay for a war which they had helped to win, and against the garrisonning of regular troops on American soil (also to be paid for by the colonists) to enforce British authority.

In 1763 the 'Thirteen Colonies' consisted, from south to north, of Georgia, South Carolina, North Carolina, Virginia, Maryland, Delaware, Pennsylvania, New Jersey, New York, Connecticut, Rhode Island, Massachusetts, and New Hampshire, the latter extending up to French Canada and including what later became the State of Maine (in 1820). Together they amounted to a settled land area of around 250,000 square miles (almost three times the size of England and Scotland) inhabited by about 1.25 million colonists of European descent or birth, with about 250,000 negro slaves – already an impressive population compared with the 7 million of Britain. The era of purely English emigration to 'The Americas' was long gone, and by the early 1770s America's population was swelled by many Irish, Scottish, German, Dutch and Scandinavian families. Since 1717, there had also been repeated shiploads of English convicts dumped or 'transported' to the New World colonies – in theory for hard labor until their deaths but more often than not, as in Australia in the following century, to begin new lives on and behind the steadily expanding colonial frontiers.

Convict transportation, incidentally, was another anti-British grievance harbored by Americans. 'What would you say if we were to transport our rattlesnakes to England?' was the famous protest of Benjamin Franklin. But it helped swell a population containing many elements – the Irish and Scots to the fore, not to mention the jailbirds – naturally ill-disposed to put up with high-handed decrees from the King of England's haughty ministers. The growing cities of the Atlantic 'Tidewater' already boasted their own aristocracies and snobberies; the colonies contained thousands of 'Loyalists' who later moved to British Canada rather than endorse American independence. In the main, however, the colonies of America contained a potent human brew which spurted to defiance under the pressure of British governmental obstinacy, misplaced contempt and woeful miscalculation. If pushed, they were ready to fight – and that included an increasingly numerous and confident seafaring population, merchant traders, whalers and deepsea fishermen, operating out of ports along a thousand miles of coast between New England and the Carolinas.

After the defeats which the Royal Navy had inflicted on the navies of France and Spain in the Seven Years War, the prospects for American colonists seriously challenging British sea power were almost ludicrously bad – when measured in terms of heavy warships, custom-built for decisive fleet actions. Of these the colonists had none, nor any experience in building them or casting heavy guns. But commerce warfare, hitting at British merchant shipping, was a very different story. Even the lightest vessel able to cruise the Atlantic, though armed with the most modest array of guns, could achieve success out of all proportion to the number of merchantmen it might capture or sink. Such attacks would force the British Admiralty to sail merchant ships in convoy, dislocating the normal pattern and profits of Britain's merchant trade and sending costs soaring; warships detached to escort convoys would be unable to blockade American ports or attack American shipping.

Commerce warfare of this nature was ideal for the Americans, being cheap and easy to wage. It could be entrusted to privateers: armed vessels manned if necessary by their normal civilian crews motivated by a personal stake in the plunder, licensed by 'letters of marque' authorising them to take prizes from a designated enemy. A commerce war waged by privateers, with the patriotism of their skippers and crews sharpened by the profit motive, could enable the Americans to wage a highly effective naval campaign as far as British home waters. If there seemed little chance of American victory in an all-out land and sea war with Britain, there was still every chance of pressurizing the powerful British merchants interest into joining the sympathetic voices advizing a settlement with the indignant colonies. Every colony from which ocean-going ships put to sea could contribute to such a campaign, which could well be a long one. Though British naval countermoves could be expected to inflict heavy losses, American shipyards had the capacity to replace every privateer captured or sunk. By 1775, Massachusetts alone was turning out 150 ships a year, and American shipbuilding was becoming more economic than in England (£2,600 for a

200-ton ship built in Philadephia; £3,000 for an equivalent vessel built on the Thames).

As the cheapest and easiest method of waging maritime war against such a powerful naval opponent as Britain, privateering could be conducted on a single-ship basis by individual colonies. For anything more ambitious – even the smallest armed squadron capable, say, of tackling an escorted convoy or raiding British island possessions in the Carribbean – inter-colonial collaboration was essential, if only because of the limited supply of guns in the colonies. Because of this, privateering remained the most important American strategy against Britain in the War of Independence and the succeeding War of 1812, 30 years later.

The events leading to the first shots in the War of Independence were complex, but may be briefly summarised here. In their first attempt at concerted action against British taxation, nine of the 13 colonies sent delegates to the 'Stamp Act Congress' which met at New York in October 1765. Unprecedented as it was, this disconcerting display of colonial solidarity achieved the repeal of the hated Stamp Act in March 1766, but only led succeeding British governments to seek other ways of showing the colonies who was master. The fateful catalyst was the British attempt to rescue the failing East India Company by 'dumping' its surplus of teas, taxed at the full rate and sold only by carefully selected agents, on the American colonies. This was in the autumn of 1773, and when the first shipment of tea reached the ports of Charleston, Philadelphia, New York and Boston it was to encounter a mixed campaign of passive and active resistance. The humiliation of being used, financially exploited to bail out a British company, had resulted in outrage in the colonies, carefully orchestrated by 'corresponding committees.' The tea unloaded at Charleston was stored in cellars, with not an ounce sold. At New York and Philadelphia the ships were refused permission to unload and returned to Britain with their cargoes. At Boston the world knows what happened: the ships were boarded by demonstrators of the 'Sons of Liberty,' disguised as Indians, and the tea dumped into the harbour. The 'Boston Tea Party' of 16 December 1773 established Massachusetts, and the port of Boston in Particular, as the center of colonial obduracy, to be chastized by economic pressure and if need be by military force.

The ensuing British 'Coercive Acts' of early 1774 were aimed at forcing Boston to make full restitution for the 'Tea Party,' but also intended effectively to place Massachusetts under much tighter political control. The Acts led to the summoning of the 'First Continental Congress' at Philadelphia in September 1775. Attended by 56 delegates from 12 of the colonies (all but Georgia), this second colonial congress rejected the Coercive Acts as unconstitutional and promised support for Massachusetts in ignoring them. Massachusetts was advized that it should form its own elected government, collect its own taxes and run its own revenue – and arm itself with a citizen militia to resist further attempts at coercion. The Congress finally drew up a 'Declaration of Rights and Grievances' for the edification of King George III, and approved an American boycott of all British goods to help this petition to bite. May 1775 was set as the date for Congress to reassemble, if American grievances had not been redressed in the meantime.

All this dictated the way in which the war broke out in the spring of 1775. Massachusetts stood out as the number-one troublemaker, and the enthusiastic recruiting of the Massachusetts militia was an obvious direct challenge to the 4,000 British troops in Boston. General Gage, Military Governor of Massachusetts, did what he could to lessen the threat by seizing all arsenals and ammunition depots likely to fall into colonial hands. One of these attempts sent 800 British troops from Boston to Concord in April 1775. On 19 April 'the shots heard round the world' were fired against 70 militiamen at Lexington, with the British marching on Concord after a heartening skirmish which had cost them one man hit in the leg, eight militiamen dead and ten wounded. The day ended with the British fighing a miserable and costly retreat back to Boston, sniped at all the way by militiamen, and an aggregate British loss of 73 killed, 174 wounded and 26 missing. American losses were only 49 killed, 41 wounded and five missing. By the end of the month, Gage's men in Boston were hemmed in by 15,000 militiamen from all over New England.

There never was a hope of confining the flare-up of colonial resistance to the Boston region. On 10 May, 170 miles away to the north-west, Colonel Benedict Arnold of the Massachusetts militia and Ethan Allen's 'Green Mountain Boys' rowed across Lake Champlain and caught the British garrison of Fort Ticonderoga completely by surprise. Two days later, 10 miles further north, Fort Crown Point was taken as well. Rough and ready though it was, this was an inspired stroke, severing the British in Boston from any hope of prompt overland relief from Canada. Gage could only hold on at Boston and await reinforcement by sea, with his troops controlling no more than the ground they stood on – and hope that the colonial delegates who convened the 'Second Continental Congress' at Philadelphia on 10 May would fall out.

But the second Philadelphia Congress did no such thing. It was confronted with a war in which the Americans seemed to have a far better chance of victory than had ever been envisaged. The New England militiamen had Gage cooped up in Boston, and the news from the Canadian frontier could not have been more promising. There was plenty of support for reorganizing the militiamen around Boston as an inter-colonial 'Continental Army'. The biggest stumbling-block, however, was the unwillingness of the other colonial delegates to agree to the appointment of a Massachusetts officer as supreme commander. This would effectively have left Massachusetts, widely mistrusted for its cantankerous extremism, running the whole show – but the problem was brilliantly surmounted by the eventual appointment of the respected Virginian, George Washington. All this took time to be hammered out; the Continental Army was not proclaimed until 14 June, with Washington receiving his appointment on the following day. Before he could even take up his duties, the deliberations of Congress were again overtaken by dramatic events at Boston.

Inevitably out of touch with the course of events in America, the British Government sent Gage reinforcements – and orders to disperse the rebels and capture their leaders. By mid-June 1775, with about 6,000 British troops ready for action, Gage prepared to clear the decks by pushing the Americans off the heights round Boston, thus ensuring the security of the only British military foothold in the colonies. But the result was the near-disaster of 17 June 1775: the Battle of Bunker Hill, which the British took at bayonet point only after the American defenders had run out of ammunition. British casualties at Bunker Hill were appalling: 1,054 out of 2,200 with at least 226 killed. It was more than enough to force Gage back on to the defensive, pleading for massive reinforcements which never came. Meanwhile, through the summer of 1775, Washington and his generals began to lick the Continental Army into a semblance of regular order, their sights set on an eventual move to expel the British from Boston.

As the Continental Army embarked on the siege of Boston, Congress – its hand strengthened even further by the object-lesson of Bunker Hill – was still prepared to try for a negotiated settlement with Britain. The 'Olive Branch Petition,' signed by Congress on 8 July 1775, offered no American concessions to King George. It was a protestation of unchanged colonial loyalty, coupled with a request for redress of grievances to bring about an end to hostilities. Determined never to negotiate with rebels, the King refused the Petition point-blank on 1 September: a stubborn, if hardly realistic, statement that Britain was not prepared to consider the faintest likelihood of ultimate defeat. The failure of

the 'Olive Branch Petition' left Congress with no option but to prepare for all-out war with Britain by land and sea. With its Continental Army already in the field before Boston, Congress authorized the formation of a Continental Navy on 13 October 1775.

Creating the Continental Navy was an infinitely harder task than shaping the Army, the raw formations of which were already in the field in June 1775. The biggest problem was the artillery shortage, which bedevilled American operations for the first three years of the war. With no gun foundries in the colonies, every popgun six-pounder embarked in a Navy commerce raider was one field gun less for the Army. Then again, it took time to conduct the necessary stock-taking of colonial vessels suitable for commerce raiding – and time was on the side of the British, enabling them to recommission a score of laid-up warships for every American raider sent out to prey on British commerce.

American colors fly over the British as the Continental schooner *Lee*, commanded by Captain John Manley, escorts the captured British brig *Nancy* into captivity on 28 November 1775. *Nancy*, with her cargo of gunpowder, was a prize of immense value at this early stage of the War of Independence.

Commodore Esek Hopkins, first commander-in-chief of the American Continental fleet. His lackluster performance contrasted ill with the more dashing successes of the American single-ship raiders and he was relieved of his command after failing to capture the British frigate HMS *Glasgow* off Block Island on 6 April 1776.

Inevitably the Continental Navy, so-called, at first consisted of a number of 'navies' raised by the different colonies. Apart from the shortage of guns, the Continental Navy suffered from an incurable dilemma. Its best privateer captains were, from the nature of such warfare, individualists, most effective when left virtually to their own devices. Congress, however, was obsessed from the start by the need to show its likeliest European allies that emergent America was far more than a mere nest of licensed pirates, hence the early attempt, late in 1775, to form a Continental 'fleet,' scraped together to make at least a show of conventional naval capacity, whose operations were always far less effective than those of individual raiders.

The fleet's commander, the first American to hold flag rank with the status of commodore, was Esek Hopkins of Rhode Island. Born in 1718 at Scituate, R.I., Hopkins had been a privateer commander in the Seven Years War and in 1775 owned a fleet of merchantmen. He was therefore qualified to command the Continental fleet on the dual grounds of previous war experience and financial self-

sufficiency, and being the younger brother of the head of the Naval Committee of Congress was no hindrance. For a flagship Hopkins was given the new merchant ship *Black Prince* of Philadelphia, hastily armed with 20 nine-pounders and 10 six-pounders and renamed *Alfred*. Her complement consisted of about 160 officers and seamen and 60 militiamen embarked as marines. 'Keeping it in the family', Hopkins' eldest son John Burroughs Hopkins commanded the brig *Cabot,* with her single deck of 14 six-pounders and 12 light swivel guns, 90 officers and seamen and 30 marines.

Apart from *Alfred,* the only other ship in the fleet with two decks of guns was *Columbus* (18 nine-pounders and 10 six-pounders). Her commander, Captain Abraham Whipple, was another Rhode Islander, born in 1733 at Providence, R.I. Getting a command in this threadbare squadron was bad luck for Whipple because he was a commerce-raiding lone wolf *par excellence*. Commanding the privateer *Gamecock* in the Seven Years War, he had captured 23 French merchantmen in six months. When hostilities against the British broke out in 1775, the Rhode Island assembly gave Whipple two ships fitted out to protect the colony's seaborne commerce. He had wasted no time in capturing the armed tender of the British frigate HMS *Rose,* the first enemy prize taken by an American warship. Though Whipple was adept at the type of naval warfare on which the Continental Navy would have to rely – hit-and-run, with maximum nuisance value – few such opportunities to shine came his way under Hopkins' command.

Captain Nicholas Biddle commanded the brig *Andrea Doria* of 16 six-pounders and 12 swivel guns, 100 officers and seamen and 30 marines. A most promising young officer, Biddle was a Pennsylvanian, born in 1750 in Philadelphia, and had gone to sea at the age of 13. Biddle was an excellent example of the fine human material suddenly denied to the Royal Navy by the breach with the American colonies, having served as a midshipman in the King's Navy in 1770. In 1773 he had requested an appointment to the Royal Society's forthcoming expedition to the North Pole, but on being refused he resigned his rank and enlisted before the mast in the bomb-ketch *Carcass*. (One of his shipmates on this abortive expedition, which returned after being halted by ice in August 1773, was the young Horatio Nelson, serving as coxswain of the captain's gig in the same spirit of adventure). When the Polar expedition returned to England in October 1773, the 'tea crisis' with the American colonies was already well advanced and Biddle returned to America. *Andrea Doria* was his first command in the service of the Pennsylvanian 'navy.'

The fifth and most junior command in the Continental fleet was Captain Hazard's light sloop *Providence,* with 12 six-pounders, ten swivel guns, 62 seamen and 28 marines. Together, the five ships of the fleet mounted 38 nine-pounders and 62 six-pounders – an extravagant concentration of guns which would have been far better employed with the Army, which in the winter of 1775-76 was preparing to batter the British out of Boston. This must be counted as a serious misapplication of the scanty resources at the disposal of Congress, which had the inevitable result of delaying the build-up of Washington's Army with no compensating gains at sea. In its anxiety to fit out a recognizable colonial fleet, Congress was forgetting that it was bound to be brutally out-gunned in any action. British frigates, the likeliest class of warship which the Colonial fleet could expect to fight, carried far heavier guns: 18-pounders, 12-pounders, on average from two to three times the weight of metal than that of the lightweight American six-pounders with their top-dressing of nine-pounders. Even a single British frigate, well handled and given the right conditions, might be expected to give a good

Below: A typically spirited encounter of the early days of the war: the capture of the British armed schooner HMS *Margaretta* off the port of Machias, Maine (11 May 1775) by 35 Patriots embarked in a lumber sloop armed with muskets, pitchforks and axes. The British captain was killed. 19 other British crewmen were killed or wounded, and the spoils included 40 cutlasses, 40 boarding axes and 40 muskets, plus grenades, pistols and two wall guns.

account itself against Hopkins' motley armada. And so it proved.

The first mission ordered by Congress for the Continental Navy was to stop the savaging of the Virginian coast in Chesapeake Bay by the dispossessed British governor, Lord Dunmore. With a handful of light warships and a force composed of Royal Marines and negro slaves enlisted on (empty) promises of freedom, Dunmore earned the nickname of 'bloody butcher' for his raids on Virginian Patriots. Unable to maintain a base ashore, Dunmore was a menance who, if not eliminated, might conceivably tempt the British into sending a reinforcing army for the subjugation of Virginia. Dunmore's flotilla was not, in fact, an objective hopelessly beyond the capacity of the Continental fleet, but Hopkins felt otherwise. He was convinced that his ships would be far better employed in beating up the British sealanes between the American coast and the Bahamas, thus forcing the British to spread their available naval force as thinly as possible.

There was no direct collaboration between the Continental Army and the Navy's only fleet in March 1776, when the siege of Boston came to an unexpectedly early climax. On 4 March Washington occupied the commanding eminence of Dorchester Heights, emplacing heavy guns (captured at Fort Ticonderoga the previous year and painfully dragged south by sledge) to menace the city and harbor. Thus surprised, the British evacuated Boston on 17 March and shipped their garrison to Halifax, Nova Scotia. While this was going on, Hopkins and the American fleet were 1,300 miles to the south, raiding Nassau in the Bahamas. With the British fleet momentarily committed to the safe transfer of the Boston garrison to Nova Scotia, Hopkins would have been able to blockade Dunmore in Chesapeake Bay without undue molestation, but the opportunity was missed.

April 1776 came in with a symbolic pair of engagements for the Continental Navy: a humiliation for the fleet, followed within 24 hours by a brilliantly successful single-ship action.

The first event took place on 6 April: a miserable encounter between Hopkins' fleet and the British frigate HMS *Glasgow*, patrolling the mouth of Long Island Sound and the southern approaches to Rhode Island. Hopkins badly needed a solid victory, to exonerate himself to the Naval Committee for not having gone to the Chesapeake as

ordered. He had won little success at Nassau, where he had failed to capture more than a small portion of the invaluable British naval stores. Passing up an action with favorable odds of five-to-one would have crowned his failure. He had little choice but to attack *Glasgow*, but he also knew that his fleet was the only one which Congress was likely to raise, and shrank from the prospect of excessive losses. The result was an inconclusive sparring-match off Block Island from which *Glasgow* escaped with comparative ease. Though his best chance would have been a converging attack by all five American ships, culminating in boarding with overwhelming manpower, Hopkins kept the range open and tried to disable *Glasgow* with long-range sniping – over-cautious tactics ideally suited to *Glasgow*, with her heavier fire-power.

Glasgow's dry record of the encounter – the only attack ever made by an American fleet on a British warship – has survived. It is notable for its detail and the surprising extent of information which the British clearly had about the American warships (or 'Rebel Armed Vessels' as they were dismissively called). All five ships names were known, with their captains, though *Andrea Doria* and *Cabot* are spelled as 'Annadona' and 'Cabinet'. The differing armaments and complements of the ships were also noted, with brief notes on the ships' appearances. *Alfred*, the flagship, was described as 'A Figure head and Yellow Sides, her Lower Deck Ports not above eighteen inches from the Water; Mizen Topgallant Sail.' Yellow seems to have been a Hopkins trademark, with *Cabot* described as 'A small white Figure head, and Yellow sides with hanging Ports;' *Columbus*, *Andrea Doria* and *Providence* were all black-painted, without figureheads.

Observers in *Glasgow* also noted that *Alfred* and *Columbus*, contrary to the normal practice of mounting light guns above heavy guns, carried their nine-pounders on the upper deck and their six-pounders below. This top-heavy arrangement, which can have done little to improve the ships' stability in a seaway, was intended to permit the nine-pounders to fire even in rough weather or during points of sailing which made it impossible to open lower-deck ports.

The humiliation of the Continental fleet off Block Island was increased when the news came through of an American single-ship victory 400 miles to the south, won on 7 April 1776. It was the first of many triumphs for

Captain John Barry, born about 1745 in County Wexford, Ireland, for whom Philadelphia had been home since 1760. He had become a merchant captain by the age of 21 and his last peacetime command had been the *Black Prince,* subsequently requisitioned as *Alfred.* Barry was commissioned as a Captain in the Continental Navy on 14 March 1776. He was appointed to command the armed brigantine *Wild Duck* which had been re-christened *Lexington,* the first of seven American warships destined to bear that illustrious name. Superbly handled by Barry, the handy *Lexington* evaded the British frigate HMS *Roebuck,* patrolling the entrance to Delaware Bay, and escaped to sea. Barry then headed south for the Chesapeake and on 7 April fell in with the British sloop HMS *Edward,* tender to the frigate HMS *Liverpool,* off Cape Charles. A communications vessel rather than a fighting ship, *Edward* had a complement of only 29 and surrendered after a running fight lasting nearly an hour – the first American prize to be brought into Philadelphia.

Though the opposition had been modest, Barry's performance had been sharply competent throughout. It was considered all the more credible that a two-masted brigantine (with square rig on the foremast only, and fore-and-aft rig on the mainmast) had captured a normally more powerful sloop. The lackluster performance of the Continental fleet appeared all the more depressing in the light of this timely demonstration of what could be achieved by American warships, and Esek Hopkins had to endure a vote of censure from Congress. He was given no further chance to redeem himself, being suspended from his command prior to formal dismissal. This unforgiving treatment of naval commanders who failed to fulfil the politician's expectations was to remain a characteristic of the American naval service. Though not without value, *pour encourager les autres,* it was not invariably successful, let alone just. In the case of the Royal Navy the British often preferred to give another chance to a man who had done good service in the past, and if Hopkins had been over-cautious he had at least kept the fleet in being. Whipple of the *Columbus,* incidentally, demanded a court martial to absolve himself of imputations of blame for the Block Island Fiasco, and was cleared.

Such were the uncertain origins of American sea power in the first year of the War of Independence: tentaive, inglorious, and yet by no means disastrous or even lacking in promise. The *Glasgow* fiasco was a sharp reminder that the Continental Navy was pitted against real professionals: the *Edward* success was a solid hint that any successes which American sailors might win would come from lucky or well-chosen encounters with opposition of suitably modest dimensions. If concentrated, vainly trying to imitate conventional fleets, the Continental Navy would be risking disaster. If dispersed in privateer commerce-raiding, it could at least continue to make an intolerable nuisance of itself. But one ugly fact was grimly obvious. Alone and unsupported, the Continental Navy had no chance of stopping the British from shipping troops anywhere they chose.

This was the hardest reality facing the American Congress as its delegates steeled themselves to sign the colonies' Declaration of Independence on 4 July 1776. At the very moment at which the American 'Founding Fathers' were signing that immortal document, British and mercenary German troops were pouring into New York, chosen as the main base from which the reconquest of the American colonies would be launched. The British build-up continued throughout July and August 1776 and by early autumn the Continental Army was confronted by about 45,000 British and German troops, 10,000 of them in Canada and the rest massed in New York. In the face of this massive new development, the only discernible American naval success was the capture of three armed transports on 16–17 June. This was achieved by Captain Seth Harding of Massachusetts in the brig *Defence,* fitted out by the Connecticut State Navy – a pinprick against an elephant.

The summer and early autumn of 1776 saw the British complete their ominous new troop concentration in New York, with the Continental Navy completely unable to stop or even delay it. Extreme measures were called for, and none was more extreme than the attempt to blow up the British naval C-in-C, Admiral Howe, in his flagship. This took place in August 1776 and, though a failure, was an historic event: the first attack by a submersible craft with an explosive warhead. The 'submarine' in question was the brain-child of David Bushnell, who had graduated from Yale in 1775. Bushnell's *Turtle* was a wooden egg enclosing a single crewman and hand-pumped buoyancy tanks by which the craft could be 'trimmed down'

U S S/M "TURTLE" 1776

just below the surface. Feeble power was provided by hand-cranked screws, and *Turtle* was also fitted with a vertical gimlet for screwing into the bottom planking of the target ship. To this gimlet was attached an explosive charge, to be left beneath the target as *Turtle* made its escape.

The *Turtle* attack was not, however, a Navy affair: it was carried out by Sergeant Ezra Lee of the Continental Army, against Howe's flagship HMS *Eagle*, lying in the lower East River. It was a gallant effort deserving of better success. Lee did extraordinarily well to fetch up under *Eagle's* stern after a downstream approach, but he was beaten by a new British 'secret weapon' for which *Turtle's* designer had not bargained: the new technique of protecting ships' hulls with copper sheathing. This defeated all Lee's efforts to force home *Tur-*

tle's gimlet and in the end he was forced to beat a retreat, chased by boats from *Eagle*. Lee managed to escape them by slipping the explosive charge and detonating it in the face of his pursuers.

The *Turtle* incident is usually remembered as an untimely freak of naval history, but it has more significance than that. In its audacity alone, it perfectly demonstrated American desperation in the face of a relentless British amphibious build-up against which available American naval resources were useless. As a might-have-been — Lee came close to success — it is on a par with wondering what would have happened if Hitler had not declared war on the United States when the Japanese attacked Pearl Harbor in December 1941. If Lee *had* succeeded in blowing one of Britain's most respected admirals sky-high it would have

The first 'submarine attack' in naval history: Ezra Lee's gallant but unavailing foray against HMS *Eagle*, flagship of the British Admiral Howe, in the East River on 7 September 1776.

Ranger's completion and fitting-out at Portsmouth, New Hampshire, before sailing for France, arriving at Nantes on 2 December.

When he met Franklin in Paris, Jones learned that *Ranger*'s arrival could not have been more timely. It coincided with that of confirmatory news of the British capitulation at Saratoga and the acceleration of Franco-American alliance talks. As the most convincing demonstration of the American will to carry the war to the British enemy, Franklin ordered Jones to raid in British home waters in the spring of 1778. This was preceded on 14 February by the first-ever formal salute of a ship flying the 'Stars and Stripes' by warships of a foreign power, rendered to *Ranger* in Quiberon Bay.

Ranger's cruise of March-May 1778 began with an abortive night raid on the Cumbrian port of Whitehaven during 22-23 April. This caused little material damage, but the moral effect of American raiders landing on British soil was naturally immense. On the following day, Jones raided the home of the Earl of Selkirk at St Mary's, planning to take the Earl as a hostage for a mass release of American prisoners of war. Unfortunately the Earl was not at home. The raiders made off with his family silver instead, but Jones subsequently demonstrated his hold over his men by returning the silver with a note of apology.

The highlight of the cruise came on 24 April when *Ranger*, approaching Belfast Lough, encountered the British sloop HMS *Drake*. It was one of the most equally-matched single-ship actions of the war and Jones fought it brilliantly, concentrating on cutting his opponent's rigging to pieces with disabling fire. Finally, when the British commander had been killed, the master of *Drake* surrendered. Jones crowned his vic-

The first 'famous victory' for John Paul Jones, 24 April 1778. At left the British sloop HMS *Drake*, her rigging already showing the effects of American disabling shot, trails her shattered bowsprit overside at the outset of the action off Belfast which ended in her capture.

Woodcut of the 32-gun American frigate *Alliance*, commanded by the unreliable French expatriate Pierre Landais during the epic cruise of John Paul Jones in *Bonhomme Richard*.

tory by fitting *Drake* with a jury rig and bringing her triumphantly into Brest – an additional humiliation for the Royal Navy in home waters, on a par with the successful running of the English Channel by the German warships *Scharnhorst* and *Gneisenau* in February 1942. From France, 200 British prisoners were subsequently exchanged for American prisoners in British hands. Deeply impressed by Jones's achievement, the French agreed to contribute warships to a Franco-American squadron to be commanded by Jones on a second cruise in 1779.

As the French authorities had all they could do to render their battle fleet fit for action in American waters, Jones got the scrapings. His 'flagship' was the old French East Indiaman *Duc de Duras*, renamed *Bonhomme Richard*. She took a year to fit out at Lorient, modified to carry the motley armament of six 18-pounders, 28 12-pounders and eight nine-pounders. Jones was also given the 30-gun *Pallas* and 12-gun *Vengeance* – both armed merchantmen – and the 18-gun cutter *Cerf*. The American contribution to the squadron was the new Continental frigate *Alliance,* of 32 guns. As her name implied, she was a reciprocal compliment to the Franco-American alignment and, to the disappointment of many better-qualified American officers, was commanded by a Frenchman. He was Pierre Landais, a French naval officer who had gone to fight for the American Patriots in 1777 and had been commissioned into the Continental Navy. His undoubted propaganda value could not, as it proved, atone for his erratic and unstable behaviour in command. Landais brought *Alliance* into Brest in February 1779, but it was June before Jones had his squadron fit for sea. When it sailed, on 19 June, *Bonhomme Richard* and *Alliance* collided heavily and the need for repairs meant a further delay until 14 August.

Safely to sea at last, Jones pressed ahead with his planned circumnavigation of the British Isles, despite the weakening of his force by the incompetence and wilfulness of his junior commanders. The cutter *Cerf* lost touch with the squadron off south-west Ireland, and never rejoined; Landais in *Alliance* kept taking off on what appeared to be his private commerce-raiding war. Thanks to Landais's refusal to co-operate, Jones had to abandon his intended entry of the Firth of Forth to raise Cain off the Scottish capital of Edinburgh. But the squadron's fortunes improved on the voyage down the English east coast, with three prizes snapped up off Flamborough Head on 21 September, and Jones remained in what seemed a promising hunting-ground. He was right. On the 23rd, the ideal target hove into view: a 41-ship convoy from the Baltic, scantily escorted by the 20-gun *Countess of Scarborough* and the 44-gun frigate *Serapis,* commanded by Captain Richard Pearson.

There was no choice but to fight, as Pearson stoutly positioned *Serapis* and *Countess of Scarborough* between this unex-

Robert Dodd's painting of the famous duel between John Paul Jones in *Bonhomme Richard* (at centre left) and HMS *Serapis* off Flamborough Head (23 September 1779). *Alliance,* firing indiscriminately into both friend and foe, is shown circling the main action at right, with the secondary duel between the American *Pallas* and HMS *Countess of Scarborough* at left.

pected enemy force and the helpless merchantmen of the convoy. Jones duly headed in to take out *Serapis,* reckoning that this would be straightforward enough with *Alliance* in support; but he was again let down, with near-fatal consequences, by the maddening behaviour of Landais. In the ensuing epic Battle of Flamborough Head, *Pallas* battered the weaker *Countess of Scarborough* while *Bonhomme Richard* and *Serapis* fought it out, with Landais in *Alliance* circling the fray and firing into both friend and foe alike.

In the duel between *Bonhomme Richard* and *Serapis,* British gunnery and seamanship told from the first. Pearson managed to rake *Bonhomme Richard,* two of whose 18-pounders burst at the beginning of the action. *Bonhomme Richard* took a fearful battering for two hours, at the end of which she was leaking like a sieve (kept afloat largely by the efforts of the prisoners of war turned loose by Jones to labor at the pumps) with only three nine-pounders still able to fire. Pearson then called on Jones to surrender – as did several of Jones's own men – only to receive the immortal defiance, 'I have not yet begun to fight!' Jones made good his words by laying *Bonhomme Richard* alongside *Serapis* and boarding: the only option left to him. *Serapis* was carried against stiff resistance, which only wilted when Landais belatedly closed and opened a devastating raking fire. At 10.30pm, knowing that he had saved his convoy and that his men could do no more, Pearson surrendered to Jones – whose first act was to transfer his men from the foundering *Bonhomme Richard* to *Serapis.*

It had been a bloody encounter, with 128 killed and wounded in *Serapis* and 150 in *Bonhomme Richard.* Jones painfully crossed the North Sea to the Texel and the temporary shelter of Dutch neutrality. There, now flying his commodore's broad pendant in *Alliance,* he managed to repair *Serapis* before sailing again on 27 December. On 19 February 1780, after evading the British squadrons hunting for him and making a cruise across the Bay of Biscay to Corunna, Jones reached Lorient. In Holland Jones had been joined by Gustavus Conyngham, who had been captured off New York earlier in the year and imprisoned in England before escaping with the help of friends in London. (Conyngham returned to America from Corunna only to be captured again, this time spending a year in prison before being re-

leased under exchange.) Meanwhile, back in Paris, Jones revelled in a well-earned hero's welcome before returning to America in the sloop *Ariel.* Congress appointed him to complete and command the Continental Navy's first battleship, the 74-gun *America,* under construction at Portsmouth, New Hampshire.

Though naturally high in propaganda value and dramatic impact, the exploits of Conyngham and Jones in British home waters had no direct effect on the course of the war in America. The spring of 1778 had seen Washington's army speedily restored from the hardships of the winter, improved by European drill, and able to take the field. The British in Philadelphia, unable to destroy Washington, were now faced with imminent French intervention; Philadelphia was therefore abandoned to permit a concentration at New York. In July 1778 the Comte d'Estaing arrived off the Delaware Capes with a battle fleet 11 strong. When he moved to New York Admiral Howe, momentarily outnumbered, kept his ships close inshore to cover the British garrison, but d'Estaing failed to combine with Washington in a joint attack on the city. The moment of danger passed with d'Estaing's removal, first to support an abortive siege of Newport, Rhode Island, and then in August 1778 to Boston. The British were not slow to profit from d'Estaing's hesitation. At the end of 1778 they took the offensive again, sending forces from New York to occupy French St Lucia in the Caribbean and Savannah in Georgia.

Apart from New York, the British had effectively cut their losses in the north and it was in the Southern States – Georgia (1778-79), the Carolinas (1779-80) and Virginia (1781) – that the war was fought to its conclusion. Apart from fleeting successes in the field, the last solid British success was the capture of Charleston on 12 May 1780, together with a squadron of four American warships (*Providence, Ranger, Queen of France* and *Boston*) trying to emulate Howe's defense of New York in 1778. The senior American naval officer at Charleston was Abraham Whipple, deploring this misuse of the Continental Navy's still-modest resources. Only one year previously, Whipple in *Providence,* with two auxiliaries, had got in among a British homebound convoy and captured ten of its ships before the escorting British warships could react. But Charleston was the last major American naval setback of the war, which was effectively won by the

The decisive fleet action of the War of Independence (5 September 1781) ended with the defeat of the British battle fleet under Admiral Graves (*right*) by the French under the Comte de Grasse.

Comte de Grasse's defeat of Admiral Graves's fleet at the entrance to Chesapeake Bay on 5 September 1781. This crucial defeat left General Cornwallis's army isolated on Virginia's Yorktown peninsula, with the French fleet to seaward and the Franco-American army to landward. Cornwallis bowed to the inevitable and surrendered on 19 October 1781.

It was clear to all that Britain had no hope of regaining her former American colonies by force, being now at war not only with France but with Spain (from June 1779) and the Dutch Republic (from December 1780). During the two years which separated the Yorktown surrender from the signing of the definitive Peace of Paris on 3 September 1783, American privateers and ships of the Continental Navy kept up the attack on

British commerce. The last important prize of the war was the merchant ship *Baille,* captured by John Manley in the Continental frigate *Hague* in January 1783. Two months later came the last clash with the Royal Navy. In March 1783, escorting a bullion ship carrying 72,000 dollars, John Barry in *Alliance* fought the British frigate HMS *Sybil,* brought down her foretopmast with his first broadside, and drove her off after 40 minutes. This action, in its sharp competence, was reminiscent of the skill with which Barry had extricated *Alliance* from attack by HMS *Atlanta* and *Trepassy* two years before.

The Continental Navy's contribution to American victory was always secondary: the commerce-raiding campaign, in which it accounted for about 200 British ships. American privateering, however, had always been far more popular and profitable than service with the Navy of Congress. It has been estimated that at the time of Yorktown in 1781 there were more Americans involved in privateering than there were serving in Washington's army. American privateers took nearly four British ships for every one which fell to the Continental Navy, estimates of the joint tally ranging from 800 to 1,000 vessels. A contemporary English estimate put the financial loss to the British war effort caused by American raiders at some £2 million.

Faced with swarming political, constitutional and financial problems of the utmost urgency, Congress had no intention whatever of maintaining a peacetime fleet of any kind. It took the States until April 1789 to agree on a joint constitution and swear in Washington as first President of the United States, and until this had been done Congress had no authority to levy taxes for such costly peacetime expenditure. Indeed, Congress began selling off ships of the Continental fleet long before the Peace of Paris was signed. The new '74', *America,* went to

The British frigate HMS *Mediator* (*left*) surprised by the French ships *Menagère, Eugène* and *Dauphin Royal* and the American *Alexander* with an American brig on 12 December 1782.

France in 1782, thus abruptly and ungratefully ending the career of John Paul Jones in American service. (He died of pneumonia in Paris ten years later, having briefly served as a rear-admiral in the Russian Navy of Catherine the Great). By the time of the Peace of Paris Barry's *Alliance* was the last warship left flying the American flag, and she was sold in 1785. For the Continental Navy, the price of American victory in the War of Independence was immediate dissolution, in the vague hope that friendly powers would in future give the United States any naval protection that might be needed.

It took little over ten years for the American Republic to accept hard reality: that the United States' essential seaborne trade would remain vulnerable as long as naval protection was lacking. From the middle 1780s, attacks on American merchant shipping by corsairs from Algiers and Tripoli – international pests swarming inside and outside the Mediterranean – left the United States with no choice but to pay the corsairs protection-money, or leave American merchantmen to their fate. Nor, when Europe became involved in war against Revolutionary France in 1792-93, was it feasible for American seaborne trade in the Mediterranean to claim the already-dubious protection of European navies. American refusal to become involved in the European conflict, signified by Washington's proclamation of neutrality in April 1793, only spelled out the fact that the American merchant marine was overdue for at least a token measure of American naval protection.

On 27 March 1794, a special Act of Congress provided for the formation of the United States Navy. Admittedly, 'navy' could be described as a grandiose term for the six frigates provided for in the Act, but there was a vital difference from the hodge-podge nature of the old Continental Navy. The new United States Navy was to be nationally funded, with an initial appropriation of two-thirds of a million dollars, not scraped together from the contributions of the individual states.

Bringing the 'original six frigates' from approval on paper into reality could well be called Washington's last great service to his country. He picked the captains who would oversee completion of the new ships – respected veterans from the War of Independence, men like John Barry, Richard Dale,

Thomas Truxton. Most important of all, it was Washington who appointed the remarkable naval designer Joshua Humphreys, a supreme pragmatist who realized that the new frigates must be able to out-sail and out-gun all contemporary ships of their class. As Humphreys put it, 'As our navy for a considerable time will be inferior in numbers, we are to consider what size ships will be most formidable and be an overmatch for those of an enemy.' Humphreys opted for 'qualities of strength, durability, swiftness of sailing and force – superior to any frigate.'

Thanks to Washington and Humphreys, the 'original six frigates' of the United States Navy – *Constellation, Constitution, Congress, Chesapeake, United States,* and *President –* were the pocket-battleships of the age of sail. Their completion was supervised by the specially-formed Department of the Navy, created with the US Marine Corps on 30 April 1798. It was none too soon. By June 1798, the United States was already involved in its first naval war.

Captain John Barry, senior captain of the new US Navy (by virtue of his services in the War of Independence) when the new service was formed by Act of Congress in March 1794.

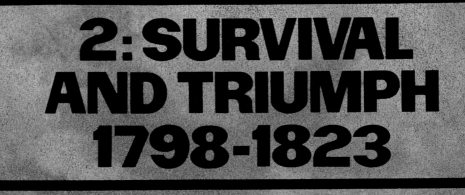

2: SURVIVAL AND TRIUMPH 1798-1823

It was certainly an irony of history that the first war which the United States had to fight was against France, the erstwhile liberator of the American colonies, but the Revolutionary France of the 1790s was a very different power from the Bourbon France of the 1770s. Luckily, the Franco-American confrontation resulted in the only form of warfare which the United States was able to wage, and no conflict could have done more to justify and expand the new United States Navy. It lasted from 1797 to 1800 and luckily for the United States was a purely naval struggle, sporadic and low key. An outright declaration of war between France and the United States was never in fact made, and hostilities took the form of mutual harrassment at sea.

The root cause of this war was French resentment and distrust not only of American neutrality, but of the successful resolution of Anglo-American frontier and trade disagreements outstanding from the Peace of Paris. These disagreements were momentarily resolved by Jay's Treaty, negotiated in London by John Jay and signed on 19 November 1794. The Revolutionary French Directory which followed Robespierre's Terror in 1795 took Jay's Treaty as a sign that the United States had become a British client in an act of 'hostile neutrality.' The Directory refused to receive Charles Pinckney as American minister in December 1796, and when he was summoned to Paris in October 1797 to smooth over the differences between France and the United States it was to receive unashamed French demands for cash payments to secure peace – nothing less than protection-money if paid. Pinckney indignantly rejected these demands while John Adams, Washington's successor as President, reaped political kudos by publishing details of the affair (the 'XYZ Affair', as it is known, 'X', 'Y' and 'Z' referring to the three French agents involved).

These events determined the diplomatic rupture between France and the United States, but a campaign of intimidation at the expense of American shipping had already begun, with several American merchant ships falling prey to French raiders by the summer of 1797. The United States Navy was in no condition to retaliate until the first of the new frigates were ready for sea in the following year. Naturally the greatest support for the Navy came from the big merchant seaports, whose prosperity was most at risk; one of the most-resented French outrages was the destruction by a French privateer of a British merchantman in Charleston Harbour. Several seaports raised funds to build warships which were then loaned indefinitely to the Navy. The most valuable of these were light frigates with broadsides about 10-15 guns lighter than those of the 'original six'. A typical example was the 36-gun *Essex,* funded by and built at Salem, Massachusetts, between April and September 1799. Pennsylvania's *Philadelphia* was another. Other seaports fitted out lighter warships, sloops, brigs and schooners, as tenders and scouts for the frigates.

As long as the conflict dragged on, the main American defensive measure was the convoying of merchant ships. As soon as *Essex* was completed and handed over to the US Navy in December 1799 she was ordered to make a maiden cruise to Batavia, Java, thence to escort home a rich convoy from the Far East trade. *Congress,* one of the 'original six', was to have gone with *Essex,* but had to turn back for repairs. This left *Essex* to become the first US warship to double the Cape of Good Hope. Her Captain, Edward Preble, had been born at Falmouth (then New Hampshire) in 1761, and had first gone to sea at the age of 16 in a privateer. In 1779 he had transferred to the Massachusetts State Navy as a midshipman. Captured in the *Proctor* in 1781, Preble was subsequently exchanged, ended the war in the Massachusetts frigate *Winthrop,* then returned to civilian life and 15 years in the merchant service. Preble's success in single-handedly bringing home the Batavia convoy in November 1800 made him a man of mark in the US Navy.

Before the undeclared Franco-American war was ended by the Treaty of Mortfontaine in September 1800, France and the United States lost about 100 merchant ships apiece in three years of sporadic raiding and retaliation. The outstanding American achievement during the conflict was the first battle fought by one of the 'original six' frigates, when the Baltimore-built *Constellation* fought and captured the French frigate *l'Insurgente* on 9 February 1799. Born at Jamaica, Long Island in 1755, Captain Thomas Truxton of *Constellation* had gone to sea at the age of 12 and in 1771 had been impressed into the Royal Navy, briefly serving in HMS *Prudent.* Truxton had been a successful privateer commander in the War of Independence, returning to the merchant service and voyaging as far afield as China

Previous page: The beginning of the end for the British frigate HMS *Macedonian* in her duel with USS *United States* (25 October 1812). *Macedonian*'s mizzenmast can already be seen floating in the sea to the right of the picture. By the end of the one-sided action the British frigate had been battered to a wreck.

before being selected for the US Navy in 1794. After his triumph over *l'Insurgente,* Truxton fought a second single-ship action in February 1800: a night encounter with *la Vengeance* of 40 guns, slightly greater than the broadside of *Constellation.* This time, however, Truxton's luck was out: he was robbed of a second victory by *Constellation's* mainmast going over the side, but emerged safely with enhanced credit from this encounter with a ship of superior force.

The foremost younger officer to make his name in the 'quasi-war' with France was Lieutenant Charles Stewart, born at Philadelphia in 1778. After first going to sea as a cabin-boy in the merchant service, Stewart was commissioned lieutenant in the US Navy in 1798, his first ship being John

Barry's frigate *United States.* Here Stewart shone to such good effect that in January 1800, aged 22, he was given command of the armed schooner *Experiment.* In her, Stewart not only captured two armed French merchantmen but recaptured several American ships which had fallen victim to the French raiders. It was a brilliant beginning to a unique career in the US Navy.

In contrast to these successes, *Constitution,* destined to become the most famous of all the 'original six' frigates, had a frustrating debut in the 'quasi-war'. Of the two prizes she took, one turned out to be a British ship, while the second proved to be a British ship recently captured by the French. Because of the overriding need to preserve American neutrality in the Anglo-French conflict, *Con-*

The spirited single-ship duel between Captain Thomas Truxton in USS *Constellation (right)* and the French frigate *Vengeance* (1 February 1800). Truxton was robbed of victory by the untimely loss of *Constellation's* mainmast, but emerged with credit from the encounter.

Prize crew away: the men of USS *Enterprise* prepare to board the battered Corsair *Tripoli* – only to be forced to release their prey under the complex niceties of international law which bedevilled the US Navy during its struggle with the Barbary Corsairs (1801-1805).

stitution was robbed of her prey, her crew suffering the mortification of having to turn a prize loose and watch it sail off under the enemy's colours.

On balance, the US Navy had stood up well to its first trial, against the commerce-raiders of a major European sea power with the bulk of its navy tied down in a major European war. It was perhaps inevitable that the next exercise of sea power by President and Congress falsely sought to apply the experiences of the Franco-American 'quasi-war' to an entirely different set of circumstances.

The problem was the old one of the Barbary Corsairs in the Mediterranean, or more accurately the easternmost nest of them: Tripoli. In May 1801 the Pasha of Tripoli, discontented with the takings of peacetime extortion, decided to boost his profits from American shipping by going to war with the United States, barely three months after the third President, Thomas Jefferson, had taken office. Jefferson's options were strictly limited. The rough-hewn American Constitution prevented him from committing the United States to war. He could send a squadron to the Mediterranean in defence of American shipping, but only with a strictly defensive brief. American warships could defend themselves and any other American vessel from attack, but could not take Tripolitan prizes, destroy Tripolitan shipping or bombard Tripolitan property, let alone Tripoli itself. The most promising bloodless way of putting pressure on Tripoli seemed to be by blockade – but without injuring the trade of Tripoli's Corsair neighbours – Tunis, Algiers and Morocco, which was impossible.

From 4,000 miles away, however, it was easy for politicians to imagine that the softest option of blockade would, after less than a year's application, end with the Pasha suing for peace on American terms. It was only after the first American squadron arrived in the Mediterranean that the men on the spot found out the hard way that any blockade of Tripoli was bound to leak like a sieve, and that more forceful measures were essential.

Command of the expedition was to have gone to Truxton after his prowess in the 'quasi-war' against France, but he turned it down in a fit of pique caused by a disagreement over the appointment of his flag captain. It passed to Captain Richard Dale, onetime first lieutenant to Jones in *Bonhomme Richard,* and justly famed in the US Navy as having been the first man into *Serapis* during the Flamborough Head battle. Dale, a Virginian from Norfolk County, was 45 years old in 1801. His command consisted of the big frigate *President,* light frigates *Essex* and *Philadelphia,* and the schooner *Enterprise.* They sailed for the Mediterranean in June 1801.

The American squadron arrived at Gibraltar in July, and at once it seemed that all the confidence had been justified. Dale's force found two Tripolitan raiders – one-third of the estimated Tripolitan fleet – making ready in Gibraltar for their next foray into the Atlantic. Dale politely informed the Tripolitan commander that he would sail only at his peril, then left *Philadelphia* to stand over the cornered raiders. When the Tripolitan crews ran out of supplies they abandoned their ships, leaving them to swing round their anchors in British custody while the Tripolitans took to the boats and headed for the North African shore across the Straits.

This was exactly the sort of bloodless happy ending for which Jefferson and his advisers had hoped, but it proved to be the last of its kind. Dale headed east towards Tripoli, looking in at Algiers and Tunis to make a polite show of force, but was then obliged to detach *Essex* on convoy escort duty and *Enterprise* to replenish water supplies at Malta.

President's arrival off Tripoli certainly made a powerful impression, and Tripolitan seaborne traffic ceased as long as she remained; but this impression swiftly evaporated when Dale, after two and a half weeks' patrolling, also ran short of water and headed for Malta. The American naval presence seemed even flimsier to the Pasha when, before the week was out, the extremely battered *Tripoli* returned to her home port. *Tripoli* had had the bad luck to fall in with *Enterprise* while the latter was still on her way to Malta, and had been captured without the loss of a single American life. But then the American commander, well aware of the constitutional shackles clamped round his country's belligerency, had turned *Tripoli* loose without taking prisoners, hostages or even loot. So far from being the hoped-for show of strength, *Tripoli's* capture and release had precisely the opposite effect. The Tripolitan Corsairs had never met an enemy like this – amateur, weak, and apparently plain stupid as far as the waging of war at sea was concerned. After the *Tripoli* incident,

Dale's hopes of negotiating from a show of strength never stood a chance, and he soon made matters worse. On his way back to Tripoli from Malta, *President* stopped a Greek ship bound for Tripoli, took off 40 Tripolitans found aboard (20 of them soldiers), then landed these prisoners at Tripoli on the verbal assurance that American captives would be released in exchange. Apart from the fact that such false assurances had been a Corsair stock-in-trade for centuries, there were no American prisoners in Tripoli at the time.

Dale stuck to his thankless task for as long as he could, from September 1801 to February 1802, but with two frigates always on convoy escort duty and one ship always in transit to replenish at Malta, this left only one ship to keep an intermittent watch on Tripoli. Moreover, by the New Year of 1802, Dale was being bombarded with unhelpful advice from the American consuls in Tunis, Algiers and Morocco, warning that the other Corsair states were preparing to raise the ante – not only with increased cash demands, but with raiders already being fitted out. Dale finally headed for home in *President* in February 1802 with his crew's commission

left with barely two months to run; the fact that the squadron's sailors had only been recruited for one year's service was the most telling proof that the problem of bringing Tripoli to heel had been grossly underestimated.

Much had been learned about the practical side of that problem, however, and Jefferson's Government prepared for a second try – this time with a stronger squadron, recruited for long-term service. With *Essex, Philadelphia* and *Enterprise* as the foundation, remaining in the Mediterranean after Dale's departure, it was hoped that no less than 12 American warships could be concentrated there. But, although Congress had empowered the President to declare war on avowed enemies of the Union, the new commodore, Captain Richard Morris, was still under orders to negotiate from strength rather than fight. He was authorized to offer up to $20,000 in securing a lasting settlement with the Corsairs.

Morris's squadron, based on the big frigates *Chesapeake* and *Constellation*, with the light frigates *New York, Boston* and *John Adams*, arrived in Gibraltar in June 1802. There the first task was to repair *Che-*

Another Tripolitan Corsair falls victim to the American armed schooner *Enterprise* (*left*) during the war with Tripoli.

sapeake's mainmast, which had split on the Atlantic crossing. At once, Morris was plunged into the morass of problems which had bedevilled his predecessor. With Morocco now peremptorily demanding the two Tripolitan ships at Gibraltar and threatening war, Morris lacked the ships with which to watch Morocco, convoy warships and settle accounts with Tripoli.

It was now clear that only a close blockade of Tripoli would bring the Pasha to heel, but this was impossible without the shallow-draught warships (brigs and schooners) which alone could venture close inshore amid the treacherous shoals outside the port. Though *Chesapeake's* mainmast had been repaired, her bowsprit had been found to be rotten, necessitating more lengthy repairs at Malta. *New York* was badly damaged by an accidental powder explosion. The squadron's manpower constantly dropped towards danger level, due to the need to keep sending home men whose enlistments had expired. The independently-minded Captain McNeill

of *Boston* remained out of touch for weeks on end. To cap it all, Congress baulked at the cost of the expedition and insisted on the recall of *Constellation* and *Chesapeake*. Morris was a dogged, honest officer of no more than average competence, when it needed a genius to overcome the problems surrounding him at every turn.

The only highlights of the cruise were provided by Captain John Rodgers of *John Adams*, born in 1773 in Harford County, Maryland. Rodgers had been Truxton's executive officer in *Constellation* in 1799 and had been appointed prize commander of the captured *l'Insurgente*. In *John Adams*, Rodgers took the first prize achieved during the cruise: the former Tripolitan raider *Meshuda*, which in the spring of 1803 made a run for Tripoli crammed with Moroccan stores. *Meshuda* was in fact American in origin – the *Betsey* of Boston, taken by the Corsairs back in 1784 – and her recapture naturally boosted American morale. But Morris failed to follow up this success. An abortive attack by *New York, John Adams* and *Enterprise* failed to prevent a shallow-draught convoy of grain ships from reaching Tripoli protected by gunboats, and a half-hearted attack on the gunboats in Tripoli harbour was also beaten off. Morris then tried negotiation, offering $5,000 for a settlement with Tripoli (he had to keep back the other $15,000 to settle with Morocco, Algiers and Tunis) but this only produced a contemptuous counter-demand for the impossible sum of $200,000 in cash, plus compensation in full for Tripoli's costs in the war.

After this humiliating rebuff Morris sailed for Malta, leaving Rodgers to maintain the blockade of Tripoli with *Enterprise* and *John Adams*. In June 1803, with a brilliant display of ship-handling, Rodgers fought and blew up a Tripolitan blockade-runner in sight of the Tripolitan army, but Morris did not exploit this success by renewing pressure on Tripoli harbour. Instead he raised the blockade and sailed for Gibraltar, only to encounter official notification of his recall. A

court of enquiry ruled that Morris be dismissed from the service – a grossly unfair sentence, with Morris denied the right to defend himself in a proper court martial. But though Morris had been cast in the role of scapegoat, Jefferson and Secretary of the Navy Robert Smith were determined to fight on, accepting the futility of the half-measures enjoined upon both Dale and Morris. Congress had also been persuaded to vote $96,000 to fit out the light warships required to close the stranglehold on Tripoli: the schooners *Nautilus* and *Vixen,* and brigs *Argus* and *Siren*. To replace Morris as commodore in the Mediterranean, Jefferson and Smith made what proved to be an inspired appointment: Edward Preble, famous for his command of *Essex* during the 'quasi-war' with France.

With *Constitution* as his flagship, Preble reached Gibraltar in September 1803. He had been preceded by the light frigate *Philadelphia* under Captain William Bainbridge, who was sent on ahead with *Vixen* to

Preble's abortive assault on Tripoli (4 August 1804) with USS *Constitution*, the only ship of force available to support the lightweight US squadron, at right. It was a forlorn hope: even the fire-power of *Constitution*'s broadside was not enough to silence the fire of the Tripolitan shore batteries.

waste no time in resuming the blockade of Tripoli. Preble meanwhile concentrated his force and entered Tangier, where he intimidated the Emperor of Morocco into agreeing a separate peace with the United States without American tribute or even the customary presents. Preble lingered to proclaim the blockade of Tripoli and set up a new cycle of convoys, then headed east – to receive the appalling news that *Philadelphia* was in Tripolitan hands. Bainbridge, chasing a blockade-runner too close inshore, had grounded her on the Kaliusa reef and had been taken into captivity with the whole of his crew, while the exultant Tripolitans refloated *Philadelphia*.

Preble's whole mission now hung in the balance, with the diplomatic triumph over Morocco abruptly wiped out by *Philadelphia's* loss. If *Philadelphia* could not be recovered by negotiation (and the Pasha dispelled that hope by demanding another American warship in exchange) she must be recaptured or destroyed. Preble took his time, maintaining the blockade of Tripoli throughout the winter of 1803–4 while he examined the problem for all angles. He negotiated the sending of supplies to the American prisoners in Tripoli, and corresponded secretly with Bainbridge (the latter using invisible ink). A shred of Credit was recovered by the capture of the Tripolitan ketch *Mastico* by *Enterprise,* the latter now commanded by Lieutenant Stephen Decatur, an officer of high ability. It was Decatur (another Marylander, born in 1779) who came up with the plan for destroying *Philadelphia* where she lay. There was no other option. With barely a thousand men under his command, Preble lacked the manpower to send a cutting-out expedition of sufficient strength to recover *Philadelphia,* and another American repulse under the guns of Tripoli would be disastrous.

Decatur's plan was to use the captured *Mastico* (now renamed *Intrepid*) to approach *Philadelphia* without arousing undue suspicion; the Tripolitans would probably decide that the weak-kneed Americans had let her go. In support would be Stewart in the *Siren,* whose rig resembled that of a two-masted ship recently purchased by the Tripolitan agents in Sicily. A storming-party from *Intrepid* would then board *Philadelphia,* set her on fire, take the boats and be brought out by *Siren.* Commanded in person by Decatur, the attack went in on the night of 16 February 1804 and was a complete success.

When the fire reached *Philadelphia's* magazine she blew up, and Decatur brought out the attacking party intact. He even saved *Intrepid,* which he had planned to use as a fireship if necessary. This feat earned Decatur immediate promotion to Captain as soon as the news reached home. But a hit-and-run operation of this nature was a far easier proposition than the close bombardment of Tripoli which Preble knew was essential, yet for which his ships lacked the necessary resources.

Preble's foremost need was for a friendly base of operations where American warships could repair and replenish without undue loss of time. With Britain and France at war again (the frail Peace of Amiens had expired in May 1803) the British at Malta had few spare facilities for the American squadron. This was a problem from which Morris, at least, had been mercifully spared. As a substitute, Preble turned to the vacillating Bourbon Kingdom of Naples with his eye on the ports of Sicily, its southernmost province. Before he could assault Tripoli, however, Preble needed the loan of gunboats and bomb vessels armed with mortars for precision bombardment, and when it came to these practical matters the professionalism of the Neapolitan Navy left much to be desired. In the end he secured the loan of eight Neapolitan gunboats, two of them bomb vessels, all manned by Neapolitan crews; but the summer of 1804 was well advanced before he judged his force to be ready to attack.

Preble finally launched his bombardment of Tripoli on 4 August 1804, pushing his gunboats inshore to close with the Tripolitan light craft and keeping *Constitution,* his only ship of force, ready to give fire support. Decatur, commanding a division of three gunboats, boarded and captured one Tripolitan vessel; in boarding a second he was momentarily overpowered, narrowly escaping death in a desperate hand-to-hand fight which became a favourite scene with American naval artists. Preble ventured inshore to sink two or three gunboats but *Constitution's* broadside, devastating though it was in frigate actions out at sea, lacked the power to destroy the all-important Tripolitan shore batteries. When an afternoon sea breeze set in, threatening to pen the attackers in dangerous shoal waters, Preble signalled the withdrawal of his force to the open sea.

Without the vital element of a landing force in sufficient strength to storm the forts, blow up the magazines and destroy the guns, there was little more that Preble's ships could do, and the Tripolitans knew it. With admirable pertinacity, however, Preble ordered his crews to repair battle damage and continue with successive day and night attacks throughout August, hoping against hope that the Pasha would lose heart and start negotiating. But it was not to be. The Tripolitans never dropped their guard enough to allow a really punishing attack to be made, and their gunnery certainly did not deteriorate. For what proved to be his last night attack (on 4 September 1804) Preble planned to send in *Intrepid,* packed with seven tons of powder charges, to explode amid the crowded shipping off the Tripoli waterfront, hopefully causing extensive damage in the city, and so cracking the Corsairs' morale. It may have been a moment's carelessness on the part of *Intrepid's* volunteer skeleton crew or it may have been a lucky shot from the shore, but *Intrepid,* which was certainly under long-range fire at the time, blew up before she was fairly into the harbor. Her brave crew — a dozen men commanded by Master-Commandant Richard Somers — had been sacrificed in vain.

It was the last disappointment for the gallant and capable Edward Preble. Though he had raised the discipline and morale of the Mediterranean Squadron to unheard-of heights, he already knew that Commodore James Barron was on his way out to relieve him, under the inflexible promotion principle followed by the Department of the Navy in those early years. These constant changes of command were naturally the foe of continuity and tended to deny worthy officers the opportunity to overcome early setbacks. They did, however, have the advantages of exposing a wide range of officers on the Captains' List to the strains and stresses of high command and, though one unfortunate by-product was constant wrangling over seniority, the experience thus gained was a definite asset to the young US Navy. Unfavorable weather prevented Preble from launching a last attack on Tripoli before Barron arrived with no less than four frigates — reinforcements which Preble would have found invaluable the month before. In mid-September 1804 Preble, already suffering from the illness which was to result in his untimely death in 1807, sailed for home.

Barron, whose most powerful ships in late 1804 were *President* and *Essex,* had entered the US Navy in 1798 at the age of 30. High-quality service under John Barry in *United States* had won him early promotion, but his performance in the Mediterranean belied his first impression in naval service. Barron had little of the natural leadership qualities of Preble, let alone the aggressive instinct and dogged endurance which Preble had displayed throughout his command. Ill health led Barron to conduct a distant blockade of Tripoli throughout the winter of 1804–5, and in the spring he handed over command to John Rodgers — the fifth American commodore appointed in as many years. It therefore fell to Rogers to handle the naval end of the amazing combined operation which, after so many previous failures, brought the war with Tripoli to a successful conclusion in the summer of 1805.

The new plan was the brainchild of William Eaton, American consul in the Mediterranean since 1799. Eaton proposed a flanking march against Tripoli from Egypt, using an Arab army raised in the name of Hamet Pasha, brother and rival of Tripoli's ruler, Yusuf Pasha. Eaton eventually raised a motley force of about 400 Arabs, led by himself with a bodyguard of seven United States Marines. Supported at sea by *Argus, Hornet* and *Nautilus,* detached from the close blockade of Tripoli which Rogers simultaneously resumed, Eaton's 'army' made an arduous 500-mile march along the coast to the Tripolitan outpost of Derna, and captured it on 27 April 1805. Two of the seven US Marines were killed leading the attack.

Unexpectedly assailed by land as well as by sea (he had no idea of the real weakness of Eaton's force) Yusuf Pasha immediately sued for peace. In an unprecedented gesture, Yusuf actualy released the captives from *Philadelphia* before receiving the token ransom which the American negotiators agreed to pay. The less attractive side of the treaty with Yusuf, signed on 4 June 1805, was the prompt American abandonment of Hamet Pasha's cause and of Eaton's 'army' in Derna (though Eaton managed to get Hamet out by sea before Yusuf's warriors reoccupied Derna). Apart from this disagreeable flash of *realpolitik,* the United States could claim to have won through to 'peace with honour' in their five-year struggle against the Corsairs of Tripoli.

The US Navy had learned much from the conflict, not only in practice but in theory. Bainbridge and his fellow captives had put their 19-month incarceration to excellent use, studying their trade with debates and lecturers — the 'University of the Prison,' in

Chesapeake's humiliation nevertheless gave timely warning of the likely penalty for unpreparedness by American warships and in the next Anglo-American naval incident of note, four years later, it was a very different story. In May 1811 Rodgers took *President* to sea to warn off the British frigate HMS *Guerrière,* which had been impressing American seamen off New York. Late on 16 May Rodgers sighted and chased a British warship which he believed to be *Guerrière* and came up with her after dark. An exchange of hails was followed by a totally one-sided gun action in favour of *President,* with each side subsequently accusing the other of having fired first. Daylight revealed that the British warship was not a frigate at all, but the puny 20-gun sloop HMS *Little Belt.* With a firepower advantage of nearly three to one, *President* was virtually unscathed but *Little Belt* was badly cut up, with 11 dead and 21 wounded. Rodgers was exonerated by the subsequent Court of Enquiry, but the 'Little Belt Incident' did nothing to modify Britain's high-handed attitude towards American shipping and neutrality.

These two incidents did not mean that British and American warships were invariably poised to fly at each others' throats; in the last five years of peace, there were occasional courteous exchanges between warships of the rival navies. In one such encounter, Captain Isaac Hull of *Constitution* and Captain James Dacres of *Guerrière,* over a glass of wine, discussed the fighting qualities of each other's ship and good-humoredly wagered a hat on which would win in a single-ship action. That friendly bet on a theoretical encounter was destined to become grim reality only two months after the outbreak of war, reluctantly declared by President James Madison (who had succeeded Jefferson in 1809) on 18 June 1812.

Though American myth naturally prefers to cast the War of 1812 as the American David again gallantly defying the bullying British Goliath, as in the War of Independence, the reality was somewhat different. In 1775 the British Government had not been willing to negotiate reasonably on every American grievance, as it was in 1812. There was a good deal more greed in the American declaration of war in 1812 than Americans like to remember. The 1810 census had shown that the population of the United States, at 7,239,881, was about two and a half times greater than it had been in 1783;

conquering British Canada, with its population of half a million protected by no more than 4,000 British regular troops, seemed an easy prospect. It was all very well for the 'War Hawks' in Congress (a term with a disconcertingly modern ring) to claim that Britain was again locked in war with the whole of Europe, and that conditions were ripe for another British humiliation. But this was a false comparison: in the early 1780s American victory had been clinched by the French battle fleet. In June 1812, nearly seven years had passed since British naval superiority had been secured by Nelson's destruction of the French battle fleet at Trafalgar.

Of course there was an equal excess of confidence on the British side in 1812. After Trafalgar, a total victory over 33 Franco-Spanish ships of the line, it was impossible to envisage defeat by a navy consisting only of a handful of frigates, without a single ship of the line. After their roll of naval victories since the outbreak of the French Revolutionary War nearly 20 years before, few Britons remembered the occasions when isolated British warships had been beaten fair and square, in untimely encounters with superior American warships, back in the War of Independence. There was altogether too much over-confidence on both sides in June 1812, and both sides soon paid for it in full measure.

Madison's administration had even less idea of how to fight a naval war with Britain than the Continental Congress had had in 1775. At one stage he toyed with the idea of keeping all American warships in home waters to serve as floating batteries, but happily Captains Bainbridge and Stewart, who happened to be in the new capital of Washington at the time, talked him out of it. Madison's biggest problem was that the mercantile states of New England, cradle of the American Revolution, were firmly opposed to war and virtually opted out of it, trading with Canada and Britain throughout. As a result the main American squadron was at New York, under Rodgers: the frigates *President, United States, Essex* (completing repairs at the outbreak of war), and *Congress,* with the sloop *Hornet* and the brig *Argus.* The nearest British force was at Halifax, under Vice-Admiral Sawyer; it was known to consist of the ship-of-the-line *Africa* (64 guns) and about seven frigates, and Rodger's main concern was to get to sea and start raiding before the British force could come south and blockade him at New York. He sailed at once, leaving Porter in *Essex* to complete his repairs.

It was a sound move, but the first American brush with the British was not propitious. Only 36 hours after leaving New York, Rodgers sighted the British frigate *Belvidera* and gave chase in *President*. The excellently-handled *Belvidera*, though damaged, got clean away to Halifax with news of the American strength, while Rodgers was left to nurse a broken leg caused by the bursting of one of *President's* maindeck guns. He then set off on a 10-week Atlantic cruise, sweeping as far as Madeira, during which no more than seven small prizes were taken.

Meanwhile, the land war had opened disastrously. Without support from New England, the ambitious triple invasion of Canada planned with such confidence by the 'War Hawks' collapsed in ruin. The Great Lakes were commanded by British flotillas. The Indians beaten at the battle of Tippecanoe in November 1811 rallied, under their great leader Tecumseh, to the British. After the briefest foray into Canada, General William Hull retreated to Detroit. There he surrendered to a handful of British regulars on 16 August, appalled by the Indian threat to massacre the 5,000 American civilians in his charge. This disaster was echoed by setbacks at sea in the first two months of the war, with *Nautilus* sailing straight into British hands off New York; the brig *Viper* was captured off Havana after a seven-week cruise with no prizes, as was her sister-ship *Vixen*.

After such a dismal prelude the remarkable run of American naval victories which began in the third week of August 1812 appeared all the more dazzling, the news of the first breaking hard on the heels of the gloom caused by the fall of Detroit.

The first victory was that of Porter in *Essex* over the sloop HMS *Alert* on 13 August. By the time *Essex* was ready for sea after the departure of Rodgers, *Belvidera* had been chased off station and New York was momentarily unwatched. Porter therefore got away unmolested on 3 July and headed for Bermuda, planning to harrass British convoys in the Caribbean. He had the luck to fall in with seven troopships escorted by the light frigate HMS *Minerva,* eluded her in a well-judged night attack, and captured a troopship with 200 soldiers. He took eight further prizes before falling in with *Alert* on the 13th and smashing her with two broadsides; the British captain surrendered to

avoid a useless slaughter. The captured *Alert,* once repaired, was used as a cartel to convey prisoners to Halifax under parole while *Essex* headed for home, taking a tenth prize before returning to New York on 7 September.

The news of the capture of *Alert* by Porter broke a week after Isaac Hull – nephew of the man who had surrendered Detroit – had brought *Constitution* into Boston with stunning news of his own: a crushing victory over the British frigate *Guerrière* on 19 August. Hull had sailed from Annapolis on the Chesapeake three weeks after the declaration of war and had headed north, hoping to join Rodgers whom he knew to be at sea. But what he actually sighted on 17 July was the British squadron from Halifax, commanded by Captain Philip Broke: the 64-gun *Africa* and frigates *Guerrière*, *Belvidera*, *Shannon* and *Aeolus*. A prolonged spell of still weather left *Constitution* becalmed just outside gunshot and an agonising three-day chase en-

Captain William Bainbridge, whose timely eloquence dissuaded President Madison from keeping the warships of the US fleet in home waters to serve as floating batteries.

sued under tow, with boats' crews trying to close within range on the British side and escape on the American. Hull, using the superior technique of kedging (winching his ship up to alternating anchors instead of relying solely on the muscle-power of his boats' crews) edged *Constitution* gradually out of reach and, as soon as the wind returned, sailed clean out of sight of his pursuers. It was a convincing demonstration of American seamanship and the impressive sailing qualities of the US Navy's big frigates.

After escaping from Broke, Hull put in at Boston to replenish the 10 tons of water pumped overside during the chase. He then headed for Nova Scotia and the Gulf of St Lawrence, beat up British shipping for just long enough to draw Broke's squadron north from American waters, then set off south to shift his hunting-ground to Bermuda – the natural tactical thinking of a born commerce raider. But on 19 August, a month after they had last been seen vanishing astern of *Constitution,* a familiar set of topsails was sighted. They were those of *Guerrière,* detached by Broke to return to Halifax. Now that prewar bet between Hull and Dacres was put to the test, with much more at stake than a hat.

Dacres' only real hope was that superior British gun drill, yielding a higher rate of fire, would cancel *Constitution's* much heavier broadside (about 684 lbs to *Guerrière's* 556). In going for speed, however, the British frigate's accuracy suffered badly, her all-important first broadside missing completely. As it happened, the decisive factors were superior American ship-handling and strength of construction; it was in this fight that *Constitution* earned the deathless nickname of 'Old Ironsides' from her apparent immunity to British shot. After a 15-minute cannonade, broadside to broadside, *Constitution* had only suffered minor damage aloft and light casualties; *Guerrière's* casualty rate was far higher, due to splinter wounds from her smashed scantlings. Her mizzen-mast was the first to go, slowing *Guerrière* and allowing Hull to swing *Constitution* across his enemy's bows, raking *Guerrière* from stem to stern with two devastating broadsides. For a moment the ships hung clipped together, with *Guerrière's* bowsprit caught in *Constitution's* mizzen rigging. The last British guns able to fire and bear started a fire in Hull's cabin, but this was quickly extinguished. Then the ships tore free, leaving *Guerrière* a dismasted, beaten wreck.

Having done all that duty demanded, Dacres wisely surrendered. The two captains met again, and Dacres offered his sword to the victor. Hull declined, telling Dacres to keep it after such a gallant fight – 'but I will trouble you for that hat.'

Guerrière was so badly damaged that Hull had no choice but to take off the British wounded and survivors (*Guerrière* had lost 78 killed and wounded out of 272) and set her ablaze. Instead of continuing his cruise and hoping to offload his captive passengers on to prizes, Hull humanely headed for Boston where he arrived, to wild acclaim, on 30 August. Viewed coldly, ship for ship and gun for gun, the *Constitution/Guerrière* fight was not that remarkable an achievement – certainly not when compared with the circumstances of the *Bon Homme Richard/Serapis* fight back in 1779. What made the capture of the *Guerrière* an historic event was its timeliness, instantly dispelling the gloom caused by the preceding run of American failures. Arguably the most surprising aftermath of the encounter was the fact that Hull was never given another fighting command, though he lived until 1843 – yet another instance of the Department of the Navy's misuse of its best commanders.

The next encounter was unique, the only occasion when an American warship has captured an enemy warship, only to be captured itself within hours. Fleeting though it proved, the new victory was won by Master Commandant Jacob Jones in the sloop *Wasp,* working the Gulf Stream trade route between Halifax and the West Indies. On 18 October Jones sighted a British convoy escorted by the brig HMS *Frolic,* commanded by Captain Whinyates. Both warships had suffered rigging damage in a storm on the previous day but *Frolic* had come off worst, having her mainyard brought down. This naturally proved a considerable handicap in the ensuing action, competently won by Jones with his superior fire-power. *Wasp* was still standing by *Frolic,* with the American prize crew making repairs in the captured brig, when the British ship-of-the-line *Poictiers* (a '74') hove into view, heading for Bermuda. Because of their storm and battle damage, plus boisterous weather conditions which perfectly suited a ship-of-the-line, *Frolic* was soon recaptured and *Wasp* taken. Jones and his men, however, were returned to New York under cartel and were received as heroes, their surrender forgotten in the light of their earlier victory. At least they had managed to tie down a vital British '74' to the tedious and distracting job of rounding up *Frolic's* convoy and seeing it safely to Bermuda.

Meanwhile two other sorties had been made by Rodgers with *Congress* and *President,* and Decatur with *United States,* with *Argus* in company. This imposing force sailed from Boston on 8 October, dispersing three days later once it was safely out to sea. Rodgers again had bad luck in not falling-in with any major convoys on a huge Atlantic sweep – south of the Azores to the Cape Verdes, and back by way of Bermuda – which lasted to the end of the year. In all this time he took only two prizes, though one of them turned out to be a bullion ship with nearly $200,000 on board. It was Decatur who had the real luck. After parting company with Rodgers on 11 October he headed towards Madeira in *United States* while *Argus* turned south to work the South American coast. Approaching Madeira on 25 October he

sighted the British frigate *Macedonian* (38), heading west to join the British West Indies Command. To Decatur's relish, *Macedonian's* Captain Carden wasted no time to coming in to attack.

Carden was foolish in doing this, for *United States* held all the hitting-power. Her broader beam made her a much steadier gun platform and her heavier guns had a longer range. *Macedonian's* only real advantages were greater speed and the upwind position or 'weather gauge,' possession of which enabled the owner to dictate the opening stage of the battle. Both these advantages were thrown away by Carden's gallant but stupid attempt to close the range at once, enabling *United States* to maul *Macedonian* to a wreck. *Macedonian* lost 100 men killed and wounded (over one-third of her crew); her mizzenmast, maintopmast and foretopmast were shot away, and 12 of her guns were knocked out. *United States* suffered only 12 casualties overall and her most serious dam-

The American sloop *Wasp*, at right of picture, crosses the bows of the British brig HMS *Frolic* (18 October 1812). The artist has missed the important fact that the beaten British ship had gone into action minus her mainyard, as a result of storm damage, but the superior seamanship of the American raking attack is still clear to see.

mand during the burning of *Philadelphia* at Tripoli. Bainbridge had hoped to sail in collaboration with Porter and *Essex,* but the latter was not ready for sea until a fortnight later. Bainbridge therefore forwarded rendezvous instructions to Porter and sailed without him, planning to work the South American trade route. At Bahia, Bainbridge left Lawrence to blockade the British sloop *Bonne Citoyenne* (which was laden with bullion and therefore sensibly declined Bainbridge's challenge to come out and fight *Hornet*). On 29 December he was cruising offshore, on the lookout for possible prizes, when he sighted the British frigate HMS *Java,* under the command of Captain Lambert.

Lambert was not on the hunt for American raiders as he was on his way out to the East Indies, carrying a reinforcement draft of seamen, naval building materials, the new Governor-General of Bombay and several civilian passengers. He was calling at Bahia to top up with water before picking up the south-west trades for the long haul down to St Helena and the Cape of Good Hope. Like *Guerrière, Java* was French-built (the former *Renommée,* captured off Madagascar in May 1811). Like *Macedonian,* she was newly refitted and faster than her more powerful American opponent. Bainbridge countered this by setting his maincourse and forecourse (the big 'driving' sails, usually kept clewed-up during action). The gamble paid off. With her edge in maneuverability blunted, *Java* was unable to get across *Constitution's* bows or stern for a raking attack; instead she was subjected to another merciless American cannonade.

This was the toughest fight yet, with *Java* shooting away *Constitution's* wheel and forcing Bainbridge to con his ship with a chain of men passing orders to crews on the relieving tackle at the tiller. Then *Java's* headsails were left dangling when her jib-boom and bowsprit were shattered – a crippling loss of maneuverability. Lambert's only chance now was to close and board, but *Java's* faltering lunge at *Constitution* missed, enabling *Constitution* to rake her twice, bow and stern. Lambert fell mortally wounded and *Java's* First Lieutenant, Chads, accepted the inevitable and surrendered. An important American bonus was the capture of *Java's* codebooks and despatches which Chads, who was also wounded, had no time to drop overside. Bainbridge himself had been wounded twice. He decided that the battered *Java* was not worth saving, and burned her on 31 December. After landing his prisoners at San Salvador (where Captain Lambert died of his wounds) Bainbridge left Lawrence to continue the cruise and returned to Boston, arriving on 27 February 1813.

Three weeks later, Lawrence brought *Hornet* into Martha's Vineyard with $20,000 in captured bullion and news of yet another victory, which he had won on 24 February. Lawrence had kept *Hornet* at the mousehole outside Bahia, watching *Bonne Citoyenne,* until the arrival of the British '74' *Montagu* forced him to escape north-east along the Brazilian coast. As he prepared to round the 'corner' of Brazil at Pernambuco, Lawrence encountered and took the bullion brig *Resolution,* then headed for the Guianas. His plan was to seek what he might devour along the Guianan coast, then try out the West Indies on the voyage home. Off the mouth of the Demerara River in British Guiana, *Hornet* had additional luck by falling in with the British brig *Peacock.*

This was an interesting battle in that both ships were armed with carronades: short-range battering guns, known as 'smashers' in the Royal Navy, useless for long-distance sparring and disabling fire. Despite the fact that *Peacock* was a far flimsier vessel than *Hornet,* the British Lieutenant William Peake displayed all the bull-at-a-gate rashness which had undone Carden of *Macedonian* in the fight with *United States.* Peake's rapid approach was suicidal. Much better handled than the British ship, *Hornet* swung in close off *Peacock's* quarter (where hardly a British gun could bear) and hammered her defenseless and sinking in less than 15

One of the most devastating encounters of the War of 1812: the attack by USS *Hornet* on the British brig HMS *Peacock* which left the British ship defenceless and sinking in less than 15 minutes.

minutes. *Peacock* sank so rapidly that she took with her several members of the American prize crew sent across by Lawrence. *Hornet's* triumphant voyage home, with 277 men aboard (127 prisoners above *Hornet's* normal complement) was made in increasing hardship due to water shortage, victors and vanquished suffering alike.

Such was the fifth and last of an unbroken string of American single-ship victories over the Royal Navy, still justly remembered with pride by the US Navy. In these repeated humiliations of the most powerful navy on the planet, it may be said that the US Navy had truly come of age. And yet, lumped together and weighed against the overall war situation, the American naval successes came to very little. They were really only a fivefold fleabite against the massive strength of the Royal Navy – now fully on its guard and hot for revenge – which by February 1813 had hardly begun to deploy its full strength against the United States. The British reinforcements already sent across the Atlantic were formidable enough. Deployed from Halifax to Brazil, it all came to 17 '74s', two 50-gun ships, 27 frigates and 56 sloops, brigs and smaller warships – odds which the US Navy, for all its mood of justified triumph, could never hope to beat.

A British blockade of increasing severity was already withering American coastal trade and communications. The Federal Government was facing bankruptcy, and it was becoming harder and harder to repair and replenish the US Navy's warships between cruises. There was no hope of any early end to the conflict, and no hope of any delivering battle fleet and expeditionary force coming from France, as in 1779-81. The only real comfort was that with Napoleon still unbeaten in Germany (despite the disastrous Russian adventure of June-December 1812) the main British Army was still pinned to Europe. Until this situation changed, the British would be unable to invade from Canada. If the United States could win command of the Lakes, the British would not be able to invade at all.

In 1813 the balance swung back in favour of the British. Rodgers sailed again with *President* and *Congress* on 23 April, but took only 12 mediocre prizes in five months. At New York, *Chesapeake* was painfully refitting after a four-month cruise in which only three prizes had been taken. Stewart in *Constellation* lay blockaded at Norfolk by a powerful British squadron; *United States* and *Macedonian,* under similar blockade in Long Island Sound, were soon abandoned and their

The unlucky ship of the US Navy's 'Original Six' frigates: USS *Chesapeake*, captured by HMS *Shannon* on 1 June 1813, under full sail.

SQUADRON OF COMMODORE BAINBRIDGE

within ten weeks. On 17 June 1815, Captain Downes of *Epervier* (Porter's former First Lieutenant in *Essex*) captured the Algerine flagship *Mashuda*, the Algerine admiral being killed in the fight. Decatur then entered Algiers harbor and dictated peace terms, including a healthy cash payment of reparations to the United States; this was paid within the week. He then moved on to Tunis and Tripoli, in each case achieving the same result. By the end of June 1815 Decatur was free to return in triumph to the United States. By waging one of the briefest, most economical and effective naval campaigns in American history, he had safeguarded American Mediterranean commerce for the first decade of peace.

Decatur's success in the Mediterranean confirmed every essential point of President Madison's peacetime message to Congress, in which Madison affirmed that 'a certain degree of preparation for war is not only indispensable to avert disaster in the onset, but affords also the best security for the continuance of peace.' He was confident that Congress would in future continue to 'provide for the maintenance of an adequate regular force,' with particular regard to 'the gradual advance of the naval establishment.' Nor were these words spoken in vain. Twenty-one years after its foundation by George Washington, the US Navy had indeed come of age and the need for its continued maintenance was self-evident.

After 1815 there could be no doubting that the future of the United States, with immediate regard to the early break-up of the Spanish and Portuguese empires in Central and South America, would largely depend on the effectiveness of American sea power. The 'Monroe Doctrine' promulgated by Madison's successor in December 1823, warning off any European inclination to intervene in the development of the Americas, was less a statement of defiance than of confidence in this new role.

Above: The US squadron triumphantly cruises past Gibraltar in October 1815 after its resounding defeat of the Barbary Corsairs.

Left: 'A View of the Gallant Action between his Majestys ship the ENDYMION and the United States Ship the PRESIDENT' – 15 January 1815. Trying to break out from Long Island Sound, Decatur had damaged his ship in a temporary grounding on the eve of the action.

3: THE UNION PRESERVED 1823-1865

the 1820s, and in this respect owed much to the calculations of J.A. Dahlgren, whose massive 'beer-bottle'-shaped guns were adopted in 1859. Once the Dahlgren gun was in service, it was only a matter of time before the US Navy followed the French and British in producing warships protected against explosive shell by armor plate. In the event, the US Navy Department ordered its first two ironclads, *Galena* and *New Ironsides,* in the summer of 1861 – only one year behind the British *Warrior* and two years behind the French *Gloire.* Yet, at the outset of the Civil War, the US Navy consisted of no more than

42 warships of all types.

This modest force had been more than enough for the US Navy's only 'shooting war' since 1815, the Mexican War of 1846-48. In this conflict the Navy's role was secondary to that of the Army: blockade and troop convoy followed by coastal support, one notable action being the forcing of the Tabasco River in 1847. (This was the war in which the US Marine Corps, serving with the Army, earned the second half of the battle honours remembered in the stirring Corps Hymn – 'From the halls of Montezuma to the shores of Tripoli'.) The main objective of the war was the conquest of New Mexico and California, and a squadron rounded Cape Horn to operate off the Californian coast. A leading light in this squadron was Commander Samuel Francis Dupont, born in 1803 at Bergen Point, New Jersey, who had joined the US Navy as a midshipman in 1815. In the Mexican War he distinguished himself as commander of the sloop *Cyane* in operations off San Diego and in the Gulf of California.

Apart from playing an active part in the crushing of piracy in the Caribbean in the 1820s, the US Navy's most enduring 'police duty' down to 1861 was the pursuit and

Above left: The steam frigate USS *Merrimack* as completed, before her half-burning and reconstruction as a mastless ironclad by the Confederates. *Below:* Union punch – an 11-inch Dahlgren gun on its slide-pivot mounting in an unidentified Northern warship during the Civil War.

interception of slavers. These operations were not limited to the African coast: they extended to the Caribbean and the Gulf, covering the slavers' home run to the markets of the Southern States. Anti-slavery patrols increased after the Northern crusade for the abolition of slavery got under way in the early 1830s – the powder-trail leading to the explosion of the Civil War. In directing anti-slavery patrols, the Federal Government had to walk on eggshells, wary of alienating either the Southern States or countries under whose flags slavers constantly sailed in camouflage. In 1847 the American Colonization Society finally achieved its aim of setting up a colony of freed African slaves on the west coast of Africa, the foundation of the Republic of Liberia. The commander of the American naval squadron entrusted with the job was Commodore Matthew Galbraith Perry, younger brother of the victor of Lake Erie.

Matthew G. Perry's greatest achievement, however, was his pair of missions to Japan (1852-53) in command of the East India Squadron, operating from Hong Kong. Perry's goal, the opening of diplomatic and commercial intercourse between the United States and Japan after centuries of self-imposed Japanese isolation, was brilliantly attained by the Treaty of Kanagawa on 31 March 1854. Much of Perry's success, which no career diplomat could have bettered, was due to the imposing appearance of his famous 'Black Ships': the steam frigates *Susquehanna* and *Mississippi,* aboard which the Japanese representatives were introduced to the delights of whisky and champagne. In his patient and sensitive negotiations, however, Perry took pains to give no impression of intimidation and succeeded by demanding nothing which the Japanese might regard as a national humiliation.

Apart from scoring one of the most important diplomatic breakthroughs of the century, the US Navy made a vital contribution to the drawing science of polar exploration. This was the first sighting and naming of the mainland of the Antartic continent on 30 January 1840 by Commander Charles Wilkes (1798–1877). He was given command of an expedition of six sailing ships, headed by the sloop *Vincennes* and lamentably prepared for the rigors of Antarctic cruising, which sailed south in August 1838. In two Antarctic forays, separated by seven months of laborious repairs at Sydney, Wilkes followed 1,500 miles of the Antarctic coastline.

But Antarctic exploration was only one task in an immensely ambitious surveying cruise which extended to the South Pacific Islands and the length of the American western seaboard. It could hardly have been completed without the ferocious discipline upon which Wilkes insisted – and for which he was repaid, on his return to New York in June 1842, by court-martial charges of having exceeded his authority. Though acquitted, his troubles were not over: he was starved of funds with which to publish the full official account of the expedition. For all that – as Mark Twain bears witness in his autobiography, referring to his boyhood on the Mississippi – Wilkes became a national hero. Fame of a very different kind awaited him in the opening year of the Civil War.

Wilkes was not unique in his contribution to the enlargement of maritime knowledge and exploration. An equally famous name was that of Lieutenant Matthew Fontaine Maury (1806–73), who succeeded Wilkes as superintendent of the Navy Department's new Depot of Charts and Instruments. Maury's genius lay in charting and oceanography. In 1847 he produced his classic 'Wind and Current Chart of the North Atlantic', and in the following year produced its practical supplement: *Abstract Log for the Use of American Navigators.* Maury's sailing directions, based on the scientific exploitation of the predictable vagaries of wind and weather, yielded impressive savings in travel time and expense. Up-dated from observations sent him by the masters of ships, Maury's *Abstract Log* was republished in 1850 and 1851, and in 1853 Maury represented the United States at the great international conference on oceanography held in Brussels.

Maury's works earned him international fame and placed the United States in the front rank of maritime science. His system did for oceanography what the Swede Linaeus had done for the classification of animals and plants in the previous century: it provided a comprehensive international framework for the advancement of science. Maury's crowning work, *The Physical Geography of the Sea,* appeared in 1855. Its practical yield was a profile chart of the Atlantic ocean floor between America and Europe, showing the feasibility of linking the continents with a submarine telegraph cable (achieved by the British in 1866). But for all his worldwide fame as a man of science, Maury considered himself first and foremost a Virginian. When, after months of hesitation, Virginia quit the Federal Union and joined the new 'Confederacy' of slave-owning states in April 1861, Maury resigned his commission in the Navy and went with her.

It was a decision taken with varying degrees of sadness and exultation by scores of other American naval officers, of both low and high rank. Some, indeed, jumped the gun, like Captain Franklin Buchanan of Maryland. Born in 1800 and joining the US Navy in 1815, he had risen to become flag captain and chief of staff to Perry during the 'Black Ships' mission to Japan, and had played a key role in the tricky negotiations with the Japanese. For this his reward was his appointment in 1854 as first Superintendent of the new US Naval Academy at Annapolis. When Abraham Lincoln was inaugurated in March 1861, as 16th President of a Union which no longer existed, Buchanan was in command at the Washington Navy Yard; his last duty there consisted of drawing up plans for the Yard's defense. Buchanan resigned his commission in the belief that his home state, Maryland, would follow Virginia into Confederacy, and was not allowed to withdraw his resignation when she failed to do so. This error of judgement went almost unnoticed in the stream of miscalculations made by the Federal Government in 1861. Another seceding Marylander destined for high renown in Confederate naval service was 52-year-old Commander Raphael Semmes, who had distinguished himself at the bombardment of Vera Cruz in the Mexican War. Under the flag of the 'Stars and Bars,' Semmes was destined to become the most effective commerce raider before the German 'raider aces' of the two World Wars.

At its fullest, fleeting strength in the summer of 1861, the Southern Confederacy consisted of 11 states: South Carolina (the first to secede from the Union), Georgia, Florida, Alabama, Louisiana, Mississippi, Texas, Arkansas, Tennessee, North Carolina and Virginia. Apart from Marland the three 'border states' of Kentucky, Missouri and Kansas, despite strong southern sympathies, were kept in the Union, so were the mountain territories which formed the new State of West Virginia. The Confederacy was formed as the ultimate protest against what Southerners considered to be a tyrannical new Republican Administration, pledged to the abolition of slavery and the consequent destruction of the Southern way of life. The

hopes of the South rested on the false belief that industrial Europe could not do without Southern cotton, and that the European powers would speedily recognise and support the Confederacy in its bid for independence.

Such foreign aid was vital, for in manpower and industrial resources the Confederacy never stood a chance against the North. The South's population was some 9 millions (of which 3.5 millions were negro slaves) against the 22 millions of the North. As for industrial establishments, the entire South could muster a grand total of no more than 16,896 against 99,564 in the North (with another 6,532 lost to the South in Kentucky and Missouri). In 1860, only one in ten of the total of manufactured articles turned out in the United States had been produced in the South. The same applied to the ships which carried the South's exports to the markets of Europe. Unless supplied from overseas the Confederacy would never be able, from its own resources, to replace the weapons and stores seized from Federal arsenals and shipyards after secession, once these had been expended.

On the other hand, the North could not mobilize all its undoubted resources overnight. The prewar US Army had barely topped 16,000 men in 1860 and 92 percent of them – 183 out of 198 companies of regular troops – were garrissoned in the West along the vast inland frontier. As for the naval front, the Confederacy's coastline stretched some 2,700 miles from the Rio Grande to the Potomac: a blockade-runner's paradise, against an enemy fleet no more than 40 strong at the outset of hostilities. The self-evident fact that the tiny US Navy could not support the Northern garrisons stranded, by secession, in Southern forts led to the firing of the first shots of the war. This was the notorious bombardment of Fort Sumter at Charleston (12–13 April 1861).

Virginia's secession followed hard on the Northern surrender of Fort Sumter, and was the first real Northern defeat of the war. Virginia was not only historically the most prestigious of the Southern States, but the most advanced in population and industry. Richmond became the new Confederate capital. The Navy Yard at Norfolk, on southern shore of the James River estuary, was hastily evacuated by the Federals but they held on to powerful Fort Monroe, north across Hampton Roads at the tip of the Yorktown peninsula. The big frigate *Merrimack* was still refitting at Norfolk and was unable

B-323

In the Civil War the North held nearly every card when it came to technological know-how. This imposing group shows Benjamin F. Isherwood (*seated at center*) with personnel of the US Navy's Bureau of Steam Engineering.

to escape to sea; the flustered Yard commander therefore ordered her to be burned and scuttled. This seemed infinitely preferable to allowing *Merrimack* to be captured intact, but it was, in fact, a fateful error of judgement. Though the flames destroyed her as a sailing ship above the waterline, *Merrimack* sank with her main hull and engines intact. Once the Confederates had raised her and pumped her out, they had the makings of a steam-driven ironclad warship – once they had found enough iron.

President Jefferson Davis's Confederate Government, taking up its duties in February 1861, was realistic enough to foresee the deadliness of a prolonged Union blockade, even if only applied at obvious pressure points like Hampton Roads. As Secretary of the virtually non-existent Confederate States Navy, Stephen Mallory of Florida was empowered to build and man ships able to challenge the Union blockade. He knew that any new warships built in the North were bound to follow the current European adop-

tion of ironclad warships, and insisted on 'the wisdom and expediency of fighting with iron against wood.' In this, Mallory was at least one jump ahead of his Northern counterpart, Gideon Welles, whose priority was commandeering enough suitable vessels to be armed as warships and sent out on blockade duties. By the time the US Navy asked shipbuilders to consider ideas for ironclads on the latest European model, it was August 1861 and the Confederate transformation of *Merrimack* was already under way.

With Norfolk separated from the Federal capital by less than 150 miles, it was not long before details of the new Southern ironclad began to filter north to Washington. Even when the wildest rumours were discounted, it was still clear that she was obviously being built for strength, and apparently more strength than that envisaged for the first Northern ironclads, *Galena* and *New Ironsides*. The Confederate Army had already shattered the first clumsy Northern invasion of Virginia, in the first Battle of Bull Run on

21 July 1861. In the shaken aftermath of Bull Run, the prospect of a Confederate ironclad able to break out from Norfolk and maybe even attack Washington was too awful to consider. The result was a panic search for an 'instant' Northern ironclad to set against *Merrimack;* and in October 1861 the US Navy decided that there was no choice but to gamble on the outlandish design for an ironclad 'monitor' (supervisor) put forward by the Swedish-born engineer John Ericsson.

Ericsson was, like Britain's Isambard Kingdom Brunel, one of the most versatile inventive geniuses of the new Industrial Age. By 1841, when he settled in the United States, he had designed railway locomotives and powered fire engines before turning his hand to screw-driven warships, naval shell-firing guns and their antidote: armor plate. In the 1840s he had built the first screw-driven warship for the US Navy (USS *Princeton*) only to fall out of favor when a gun designed (but not built) by him burst on her trials, killing two Cabinet ministers.

Still under a cloud in 1861, Ericsson was nevertheless consulted by Cornelius Bush-nell, the Connecticut shipbuilder who had won the contract for *Galena.* It was Bushnell who acted as go-between for Ericsson, urging the Navy Department to consider a cardboard model which looked like nothing on earth. It had no masts; it had no apparent freeboard; it had no conventional broadside of guns, but only two guns in a rotating pillbox turret. All the experts laughed Ericsson's model to scorn. But none of them could produce so much as a sketch for an ironclad which could be built in as little as 100 days (as Ericsson insisted was possible for his 'monitor'), and so wipe out the Confederate lead with *Merrimack.* It was to give the US Navy *something* with which to fight *Merrimack* that Ericsson was contracted, in October 1861, to build USS *Monitor.*

By this time the Confederate Navy had already given embarrassing proof of what it could do with conventional craft. CSS *Sumter* was the former mail packet *Havannah,* armed as a commerce raider with four 24-pounders and an 8-inch swivel gun. Under Commander Raphael Semmes, she slipped out of New Orleans in June 1861, easily dodging the lone USS *Brooklyn* patrolling

Forging the new steam-and-iron Navy – factory chimneys and gaunt new hulls at Washington Navy Yard, DC, about 1862.

the Mississippi approaches, and set off on a six-and-a-half-month commerce-raiding cruise through the Caribbean and Atlantic in which 17 Northern merchantmen were destroyed. By January 1862 the Confederacy had produced a commerce-raiding 'ace' fit to rank with the American naval heroes of the War of Independence and the War of 1812.

Moreover, by the fifth month of *Sumter's* cruise the Confederacy's wildest dream seemed on the verge of realization. The Northern blockade had laid heavy hands on a British ship, bringing the United States and Britain to the brink of war. The culprit was Captain Charles Wilkes, the former Antarctic hero. He had been at Norfolk when Virginia seceded, waiting to take command of *Merrimack;* instead he had had the job of burning her, before being appointed to *San Jacinto* and sent down to the Caribbean to hunt for Confederate blockade-runners. On 8 November 1861 Wilkes had stopped the British mail steamer and arrested two Confederate envoys (Senators James Mason and John Slidell) on their way to plead the Confederate cause in France and Britain.

It has been said that the absence of an Atlantic telegraph cable, providing a natural 'cooling-off period,' kept the peace; this was precisely the sort of act for which the two nations had gone to war in 1812. On both sides of the Atlantic the popular press yelped war-talk, hailing Wilkes as a hero in the United States and calling for direct action to avenge the insult in Britain. The two Governments showed far more sense, Whitehall accepting that Wilkes had not been carrying out deliberate orders and Washington releasing Mason and Slidell without a formal apology to Britain (the arrest having been disavowed). As for Wilkes, he was promoted Acting Rear-Admiral in 1862 and kept in the Caribbean to keep up the pressure on Confederate blockade-runners. (Undoubted success in this role did not, however, save him from court-martial two years later and conviction for 'disobedience, disrespect, insubordination, and conduct unbecoming an officer'. After one year's suspension from duty he was finally retired with the rank of rear-admiral in 1866.)

The New Year of 1862 therefore came in with Confederates beginning to accept that they were on their own, forced to save themselves by their own exertions without foreign aid; and the building race between *Merrimack* and *Monitor* continued apace. Inventing and correcting as he went along,

Ericsson proved as good as his word: *Monitor* was launched at New York on 30 January 1862. She was the first wartime naval achievement of the Industrial Revolution, her construction having been farmed out to different firms for the separate manufacture of hull, engines, turret, and armor plate – a facility denied the Confederacy, with its lack of industrial plant. Not surprisingly, *Monitor* was riddled with teething troubles (mostly concerned with the steering gear) and she was not ready to be towed down to Hampton Roads until 6 March. This enabled *Merrimack* (now re-christened CSS *Virginia*) to beat *Monitor* into action by less than a day.

The ungainly Southern ironclad had been rebuilt with a massive angled penthouse running fore and aft, of heavy timbers sheathed in armor plate (the latter mostly contrived from railway iron). She carried eight guns in broadside (four per side) plus a bow and stern gun, each of the latter swiveled for a choice of fire through three ports. Unlike *Monitor*, *Virginia* had been given an armored spur with which to ram enemy ships below the waterline: an attack technique wholly unsuited to sailing warships. *Virginia* was so unweatherly that she could only operate safely in a calm; a storm on 7 March (which all but sank *Monitor* on her way down from New York) delayed her first sortie by a day. But on 8 March 1862 *Virginia* became the world's first ironclad to go into action. Under Captain Franklin Buchanan, commanding the Confederate James River Flotilla, *Virginia* lumbered across Hampton Roads to sink the becalmed sailing sloop USS *Cumberland* with a ramming attack, then turned on the nearby frigate *Congress* and set her ablaze with shellfire and red-hot shot.

All this was accomplished in the teeth of point-blank fire from the Union ships and their covering shore batteries. *Virginia's* armor survived the lot, though Buchanan (venturing outside for a better view) was wounded by a rifle bullet; he was replaced in command by Lieutenant Jones. With evening approaching and the tide on the ebb, restricting *Virginia's* already limited maneuverability, Jones prudently decided to withdraw for the night and finish off *Minnesota, St Lawrence* and *Roanoke* on the morrow. As night fell, however, the insignificant shape of *Monitor* came steaming in past Fort Monroe, and daybreak on 9 March found her poised to defend *Virginia's* intended victims.

The extraordinary fight between *Virginia*

and *Monitor* on the forenoon of 9 March 1862, the first-ever battle between ironclad warships, ended with neither ship having inflicted vital damage on the other. *Monitor's* heavier guns were frustrated by *Virginia's* sloping armor. Though the two ships battered each other for three hours, there was only one serious casualty: Lieutenant John Worden, commander of *Monitor*, Momentarily blinded by a direct hit on the observation-slit through which he was peering. Until Lieutenant Greene took over command and brought *Monitor* back into the fight, *Virginia* seemed on the point of adding *Minnesota* to her tally of victims, but prudently retired again with the ebb of the tide, rather than risk being stranded. On balance *Virginia* had taken the heavier damage, with the muzzles of two guns shattered, her tall stack shot away and a leak in the bows from the loss of her ram during the earlier attack on *Cumberland*, aggravated by an abortive attempt to ram *Monitor*. Though *Monitor* had undoubtedly frustrated *Virginia's* attempt to break the Union blockade of the James River, the Battle of Hampton Roads ended in a stalemate which seemed destined to last as long as the two ironclads confronted each other.

The stalemate was abruptly broken in just over two months by the movement of the land armies, beginning on 4 April with a Northern advance on Richmond up the Yorktown peninsula. This forced the Confederates to evacuate first Yorktown and then Norfolk (4-10 May 1862). When it proved impossible

to move *Virginia* up the James to defend Richmond, she was set on fire and blown up by her crew on 11 May. Four days later her gunners helped repel an attempt by the US Navy to force open a direct route to Richmond up the James by bombarding and passing Fort Darling. The Northern flotilla consisted of *Monitor*, the new ironclad *Galena* and three gunboats, and its defeat revealed the limitations of ironclads when opposed by well-emplaced shore batteries. Hit 43 times, *Galena* was reduced to a wreck, her frail 4-inch armor shattered. She never saw service as an ironclad again. *Monitor* again came through unscathed, but her guns could not be elevated enough to silence the Confederate fire.

Richmond was saved by Robert E. Lee's victory in the Battle of the Seven Days (25

Above: Union gunboat USS *Choctaw* off the battered city of Vicksburg in 1863. *Below:* The distinctive pill-box turret of a Northern monitor: USS *Lehigh* in the James River, spring 1863.

Distinctive features of the river gunboats during the Civil War were the sloping, armored sides of the casemate and broadside guns protected by armored ports. *Right:* The crew of USS *Cincinnati* take advantage of a quiet spell and good laundry-drying weather. *Below:* USS *Cairo* in more martial guise, 'showing her teeth' for the camera.

June-1 July 1862), after which the Union field army was withdrawn from the Yorktown Peninsula. Apart from a two-month withdrawal to New York for repairs, *Monitor* remained on the lower James River until December 1862. On the last day of the year, while attempting another sea voyage to join the naval blockade of Wilmington, North Carolina, *Monitor* foundered and sank off Cape Hatteras – a sad end to an astonishing operational career which . had changed warship design for good.

Whilst 1862 was a year of repeated Union frustration and defeat in the East, it was a very different story in the West. There the US Navy, though operating hundreds of miles from salt water, played a vital role in helping slice the Confederacy in two down the line of the Mississippi. The armored river gunboats of the North were essential in overwhelming or by-passing the Confederate strongpoints barring the southward Union advance.

Building the Union gunboat fleet was, like the breakneck construction of *Monitor*, another remarkable demonstration of the North's industrial muscle. It was achieved largely by the organising genius of millionaire industrialist James B. Eads, who masterminded the construction of seven new ironclad gunboats well within the promised 65 days. These were *St Louis, Carondelet, Cincinatti, Louisville, Mound City, Cairo* and *Pittsburgh*, built piecemeal in timber yards, foundries and workshops scattered across eight of the Northern states. Eads then added two more gunboats, one converted from a river salvage boat (*Benton*) and one

UNITED STATES MISSISSIPPI GUN-BOATS BEING BUILT AT CARONDELET, NEAR ST. LOUIS, MISSOURI.
[SKETCHED BY ALEXANDER SIMPLOT.]

Above: Mass production of Mississippi gunboats at the Eads works, Carondelet, Missouri, in October 1861. *Right:* The screw, unarmored under-hull and waterline armor belt of USS *Dictator*, probably photographed shortly before her launch on 26 December 1863 – Delameter Iron Works, New York.

from a ferry (*Essex*). All were broad in the beam, flat-bottomed stern-wheelers, known generically as 'Pook's Turtles' after Samuel M. Pook, the naval architect working in harness with Eads. Commanded by Flag Officer Andrew Foote, the Northern gunboat fleet mustered at Cairo, Illinois, to support the first drives against the Confederate river strongholds in the New Year of 1862.

The gunboats got off to a resounding start with the shattering bombardment which assisted General Ulysses S. Grant to capture Fort Henry on the Tennessee River on 6 February 1862. They moved to the Cumberland River to spearhead Grant's follow-up capture of Fort Donelson on 16 February, then returned to Cairo to make repairs before tackling the first major barrier on the Mississippi: 'Island Number 10', north-western bastion of the Tennessee frontier. Here, frustrated by the well-sited Confederate batteries, the Union advance stuck until *Carondelet* ran the gauntlet on the night of 4-5 April and silenced the guns preventing Union troops from crossing to surround the fortress. This early winning of Northern supremacy on the central Mississippi was followed at once by one of the US Navy's finest feats of the Civil War: nothing less than the capture of New Orleans, the Confederacy's second city.

The victor of New Orleans was 61-year-old Flag Officer David Glasgow Farragut, a veteran of the War of 1812 who had sailed the Pacific under Porter in *Essex,* and had been captured in her. The plan to take New Orleans was formed after the first Northern footholds on the Confederate Atlantic coast had been won with comparative ease: Hatteras Inlet (29 August 1861) and Port Royal (7 November 1861), followed by Roanoke Island on 7 February 1862. To tackle New Orleans, Farragut was given 10,000 troops and a fleet consisting of eight steam-powered warships,

Victor of New Orleans and Mobile Bay: Admiral David G. Farragut strikes a suitably heroic pose beside the wheel of his flagship, USS *Hartford*, at Mobile in 1864. With Farragut is the bearded Captain Percival Drayton, USN.

Opposite, below:
Northern and Southern gunboats clash at Memphis, 6 June 1862. At center, the USS *Monarch* rams the Confederate *General Beauregard*; the Confederate *General Price* can be seen at left, with the Confederate flagship *Little Rebel* in the background.

nine gunboats and a flotilla of mortar schooners. None of these were ironclads, and when Farragut heard that the Confederates were building two large ironclads (*Louisiana* and *Mississippi*) for the defense of New Orleans, he decided to attack before they were ready. Farragut was not deterred by the pair of forts, Jackson and St Philip, commanding the channel leading north to New Orleans; he intended to pass them, not match them in fire-power, and he did just that. Within 24 hours after fighting his way past the forts, Farragut's ships anchored off the New Orleans waterfront to receive the surrender of the defenseless city on 25 April 1862.

By the end of June 1862 Fort Pillow and Memphis had followed New Orleans, Island No. 10 and Forts Henry and Donelson, and Confederate control of the Mississippi had shrunk to the three-mile waterfront of Vicks-

burg, Mississippi. Farragut had cruised up from New Orleans to join hands with the Northern gunboats, now commanded by Flag Officer Charles H. Davis – but, even when the two forces joined above Vicksburg, they proved unable to capture the town without a powerful land army attacking from the east. Silencing the guns of Vicksburg on their commanding bluffs above the town was a task beyond Farragut's warships and gunboats. As *Monitor* had discovered at Fort Darling on the James River, two months before, not even the most powerful ironclad could neutralize positions sited on high ground beyond the limited elevation of its guns. In October 1862 Farragut, now a rear-admiral, withdrew his seagoing ships to New Orleans. His replacement as the new Flag Officer on the Mississippi was the commander of his mortar boats during the assault on New Orleans: David Dixon Porter, son of Farragut's old commander in the War of 1812.

The fate of the war hung in the balance from the high summer of 1862 to that of 1863. The string of famous Confederate land victories won in the East by Robert E. Lee and 'Stonewall' Jackson, went hand in hand with a succession of failures for the US Navy. On the high seas, Raphael Semmes was on the loose in a new Confederate raider, CSS *Alabama,* secretly built in Britain, which began a remarkable two-year cruise in August 1862 and destroyed 20 US ships in her

The Confederate ironclad Arkansas, at center, running through the Union fleet off Vicksburg, 15 July 1862.

Federal Ram Queen of the West disabled.   Rebel Ram General Price.   Rebel Flag-ship Little Rebel.   Federal Gun-boat running down the Beauregard.

THE GREAT NAVAL BATTLE BEFORE MEMPHIS, JUNE 6, 1862.—SKETCHED BY MR. A. SIMPLOT.—[SEE PAGE 410.]

first two months of operations alone. In January 1863 she sank the Union gunboat *Hatteras* off Galveston before extending her hunting grounds to the South Atlantic, Indian Ocean and China Sea – a range remarkable by the standards of the day, and destined not to be surpassed until the disguised German merchant-raiders of the two World Wars. In March 1863 Porter's gunboats, frankly attempting the impossible, failed to break through to the upper Yazoo River in Vicksburg's rear by forcing a channel from bayou to vegetation-clogged bayou. In the following month Rear-Admiral Samuel Du Pont, victor at Hatteras Inlet in November 1861, tried to take Charleston with a bold frontal assault by nine ironclads, seven of them turretted monitors. Though their armor stood up well to a formidable hammering by the guns of Fort Sumter and the other Charleston forts – they fired an astonishing 2,209 rounds to only 139 from Du Pont's ships – Du Pont was forced to order a humiliating withdrawal after two hours. Like Vicksburg, Charleston was a target beyond the US Navy's capacity and held out

until invested from the landward by the Army.

After the tide turned for good with the twin Confederate defeats at Vicksburg and Gettysburg in July 1863, the biggest threat to units of the US Navy was posed by weapons born of desperation: the mine and the torpedo (both referred to as 'torpedo'). Torpedoes of the Civil War were of the spar variety: extended from the bow of a fast boat, manned by what amounted to a suicide crew. The first Confederate torpedo attack was against *New Ironsides* off Charleston in October 1863, but though the ironclad's plates were started by the explosion the ship survived. It was a very different story with the wooden-hulled *Housatonic*, ripped open and sunk by a spar torpedo on 7 February 1864. A new factor had entered naval warfare. It was one which the Confederate Admiral Buchanan hoped would keep Farragut's fleet out of Mobile Bay, the last Confederate naval base on the Gulf by the summer of 1864.

Well aware of the 'torpedo' menace, Farragut was more concerned with running his

Map of the Battle of Mobile Bay (5 August 1864) showing Farragut's line of approach and *(inset)* the massive concentration of fire-power brought to bear on the Confederate ironclad *Tennessee*.

fleet in past Fort Morgan, guarding the entrance to the Bay. He used his four monitors as a line-ahead screen for his wooden ships, which he had lashed together in pairs for safety. This level-headed deployment had the desired result, with the monitors drawing the bulk of Fort Morgan's fire during the critical entry to Mobile Bay – but the Union fleet was thrown into momentary disarray when the leading monitor *Tecumseh* hit a 'torpedo' and sank with 93 of her crew of 114. Farragut rose splendidly to the crisis, giving the US Navy a watchword fit to rank beside 'Don't give up the ship!' and 'I have not yet begun to fight!' 'Damn the torpedoes!' he barked. 'Full speed ahead!'

Having failed to keep Farragut's fleet out of the Bay, Buchanan's last hope was the prowess of his flagship *Tennessee,* the South's last heavy ironclad – but she stood no chance against the terrible combined pounding, at point-blank range, by the Union monitors *Winnebago* and *Chickasaw*. After a heroic fight, with her steering gone and her armor

being blown off in great chunks, *Tennessee* surrendered and the battle was over.

The Battle of Mobile Bay on 5 August 1864 was the last fleet action of the American Civil War. It was fought two months after *Alabama* was finally caught off Cherbourg by Captain John A. Winslow of USS *Kearsarge,* and sunk after a no less dramatic single-ship action. Extraordinary honors

"BROOKLYN."   "ITASCA."   "RICHMOND."   "HARTFORD."   "CHICKASAW."

"TENNESSEE."   FORT MORGAN.

NDER OF THE "TENNESSEE," BATTLE OF MOBILE BAY.

were paid to Winslow by a grateful government, as had been paid to Britain's Captain Broke after his capture of USS *Chesapeake* in 1813. Apart from an immediate promotion to Flag Officer and unusually early postwar advancement to Rear-Admiral, Winslow was ordered to be kept on the active list for the rest of his life.

When Lee's Army surrendered to Grant at Appomattox on 9 April 1865, the US Navy could claim to have played a full and varied part in the victory of the Union. Indeed, no other Navy had ever been forced to undergo a greater transformation in a mere four years of war. It now remained to be seen how much of this impetus would be lost, and how much retained, as the battle-scarred American nation prepared to heal its wounds in peace.

Position of the ships at the moment of *Tennessee*'s surrender, hemmed in on all sides.

81

4: IRONCLADS AND DREADNOUGHTS 1865-1918

Below: Paving the way to an American 'Two-Ocean' battle fleet – the coastal battleship USS *Iowa* (BB.4) as completed, before a towering 'cage' mainmast was installed aft of the stacks. Launched in 1896, *Iowa* served through the First World War in the training role, being expended as a gunnery target in 1923.

Squadron, with other naval bases subsequently added at Bremerton, Puget Sound, to the north and finally at San Diego to the south. By the middle 1890s, the transformation of the US Navy into a permanently 'two-ocean' navy was an accomplished fact.

Though the enduring years of peace saw the lead in warship and gunnery design recross the Atlantic to Europe, this also had direct advantages for the US Navy. With money kept tight by Congress, American designers were denied the costly interim experiments made by their European counterparts. British and French designers came up with many a weird and wonderful hybrid design between 1865 and 1885, as the full sailing-ship rig of masts and yards passed into final obsolescence. The US Navy Department could afford to lie back and opt for the best of the European designs for application to American needs – and this by no means implied excessive reliance on European experience.

One of the greatest American naval assets in these years was the remarkable shipbuilder Charles H. Cramp (1828-1912), who gave the US Navy an invaluable continuity in ship design from the ironclads of the Civil War to the battleships and cruisers of the

Dreadnought era. Cramp had given the US Navy its first seagoing ironclad, *New Ironsides*, in 1862; 30 years later, with *Indiana*, *Massachusetts*, and *Iowa* (BBs. 1-3, laid down 1891-93) he produced the first modern American battleships. These were only the precursors of four more battleships built at Cramp's Philadelphia yard before his death: *Alabama* (BB.8), *Maine* (BB.10), *South Carolina* (BB.26), and *Wyoming* (BB.32) – the latter a full-blown Dreadnought with twelve 12-inch guns.

No less important, though overshadowed in the prevailing anxiety not to be outstripped in the development of conventional sur-

Above: A typical cruiser of the post-Civil War years – USS *Richmond* as she looked after receiving an 8-inch rifled pivot gun in her refit of 1877-78, and before her bridge was rebuilt forward of the stack in her refit of 1884-87.

Right: Heavy metal for the Pacific theater – 'Indiana' class battleship USS *Oregon* (BB.3) sets out from New York on the long haul round Cape Horn, bound for Manila in the Philippines, on 12 October 1898. Like her sister-ships *Indiana* and *Massachusetts*, she carried a main armament of four 13-inch guns in centerline turrets, with a secondary armament of eight 8-inch guns.

ammunition explosion (a tragedy known to all battleship navies down to and including the Second World War), but Hearst's newspapers shrieked accusations of Spanish sabotage. The fact that Spain apologized unreservedly and offered all sympathy, plus practical suggestions for resolving the crisis, went for nothing: the real American goal was not Cuba but the Spanish Philippines, on China's doorstep. On 21 April 1898, President William McKinley approved the Congressional resolution for armed intervention.

Meanwhile, bellicose Assistant Navy Secretary 'Teddy' Roosevelt had, without any authorization, briefed the commander of the US Pacific Squadron to move from Hawaii to Hong Kong. Thence, as soon as he heard that war with Spain had been declared, he was to descend on Manila and attack the Spanish fleet. Commodore George Dewey (1827-1917) had served under Farragut during the capture of New Orleans in 1862 and had a distinguished Civil War career. After running the gauntlet of Forts Jackson and St

Philip he was not deterred by the prospect of the Spanish batteries commanding Manila Bay, and sailed from Hong Kong with his six cruisers on 25 April. Shortly after midnight on 1 May, Dewey sailed past the outermost forts, ignored the shore batteries and headed straight for the ramshackle fleet.

Rarely, if ever, can American warships have had softer opponents. Admiral Montojo had seven ships in all, only three of them armored, and one a hulk which could only move under tow. So far from being drawn up in line of battle, Montojo had anchored close inshore to save as many of his crewmen as possible when the moment came to abandon ship. Dewey's chosen tactics were redolent of Civil War ironclad experience. Instead of anchoring to slug it out ship to ship, he made five slow runs past his victims, retiring to send the American crews to breakfast to give the smoke a chance to clear. It was typical of this war that Dewey went into US naval legend for his perfectly natural order to his gunnery officer on the eve of the first attacking pass: 'You may fire when you are ready, Gridley.' By noon, what was left of Montojo's fleet surrendered, Spanish casualties totaling 381 in exchange for eight Americans lightly wounded and an overweight American chief engineer dead from heatstroke after collapsing below decks.

The Battle of Manila Bay established Dewey as the greatest American naval hero since Farragut, but ironically it was not for the battle but for its aftermath that Dewey deserved the fullest praise. He had no troops. He could not land to capture Manila. All he could do was stay on station, waging a magnificent game of bluff, until General Merritt arrived with an American expeditionary force. It took *14 weeks* before the troops arrived; landed; fought a brisk skirmish (six Americans and 49 Spaniards dead); and accepted the surrender of Manila on 13 August. The hardest fighting in this 'splendid little war' (as Secretary of State John Hay expressed it to Roosevelt) was in the Cuban theater, where 509 American troops

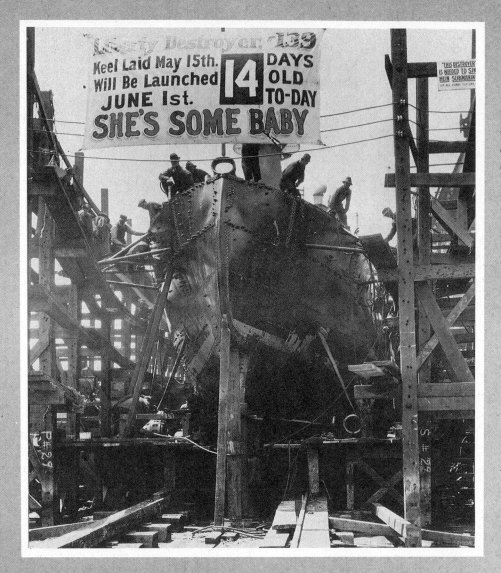

The fact that Anglo-American naval collaboration worked out superbly in 1917-18 was due to the high tact and ready diplomacy displayed by the American naval commanders in European waters. Rear-Admiral William S. Sims (1858-1936) was 'Commander of the US Naval Forces Operating in European Waters.' His task, coming under the British Admiral Sir Lewis Bayly, based on Queenstown, Ireland, was to collaborate in the provision of Atlantic convoy escorts against the U-boats. Admiral Hugh Rodman (1959-1940) commanded the American Dreadnought battle squadron which joined the ranks of the British Grand Fleet, under the overall British command of Admiral Sir David Beatty. As an element of the Grand Fleet the American force was designated '6th Battle Squadron,' adopting British methods of signalling and fire control. The original battleships of 6th Battle Squadron (BatDiv 6, in US naval parlance) were *New York* (flag), *Florida*, *Wyoming* and *Delaware*.

It was with the fully-justified pride in faith kept and a job well done that Rodman's squadron deployed with its Grand Fleet comrades, on 21 November 1918, to receive the German High Seas Fleet as it came steaming duly west to surrender off the Firth of Forth. The German naval threat to American sea power had been destroyed – to all appearances, for ever. The Japanese naval threat continued to grow. How the peacetime naval powers could achieve a mutually satisfactory balance of strength – assuming such a feat were possible – remained to be seen.

Opposite, top: The amazing capacity of American warship production. In the summer of 1918, less than three weeks from laying-down to launch, the destroyer DD.139 (USS *Ward*) prepares to take the water.

Above: Scene of bleak discomfort on the exposed bridge of a US destroyer in the First World War.

Below: Over there – the destroyer USS *Stockton* (DD.73) in British waters.

After the defeat of Germany and her allies in November 1918, the future of the US Navy was more uncertain than at any other time in its history. The US Navy's two previous trials – in the Spanish-American War of 1898 and the American Civil War of 1861-65 – had ended with the enemy prostrate and all objectives for the conceivable future secured. This was not the case in 1918, and even the scuttling of the surrendered German fleet in Scapa Flow in the following April failed to dispel the clouds. It was true that one of the US Navy's potential rivals, that of Germany, had been liquidated. But that of Japan had not only emerged from the First World War in a much stronger strategic position, but had already embarked on a new spate of naval construction which could only be aimed at eclipsing American sea power in the Pacific.

Under the terms of the Treaty of Versailles, Germany was to be stripped of all her global colonies. These were to be shared out among the victorious powers and organised as mandates under supervision of the newly-formed League of Nations. In the case of Germany's colonies in the western and southern Pacific, these were divided north and south of the line of the Equator between the Japanese and British Empires, Japan took the Marianas (with the exception of American-held Guam), the Palaus, Carolines and Marshalls. The Bismarck Archipelago – New Britain and New Ireland – passed into Australian control, Samoa into that of New Zealand.

The former German presence in the western Pacific had been tolerable to the United States because it was not sustained by a powerful German Pacific Fleet. But the transfer of these possessions to Japan was a very different story, creating as it did an enormous bastion of Japanese-controlled ocean stretching from the Japanese home islands south to the Equator. Viewed in the light of possible future hostilities between the United States and Japan, the situation could not have been less promising for the United States. The Philippines now lay isolated to the west of Japan's new island empire; Guam lay, completely surrounded by Japanese possessions, plumb in the middle; and the widely-separated American-held islands of Marcus, Wake, Midway, and the Hawaiian group lay to the east. The strategic possibilities in the western Pacific, after the postwar settlement came into effect, amounted to all weakness for the Americans

and all strength for the Japanese.

Times had also changed since Japan had won the reputation as the plucky underdog which had made good against the might of Tsarist Russia in the war of 1904-5. But this approving reputation had begun to wane with the unabated growth of the Japanese Navy in the decade before the First World War. The British had begun to have second thoughts about their former client (most of the Japanese fleet which had shattered the Russians at Tsushima in 1905 was of British manufacture or design) when Japan ordered a new battle-cruiser, *Kongo*, in 1911. No navy in the world had yet moved up from the 12-inch gun to the 14-inch; *Kongo* had eight 14-inch guns, 10 inches of armor and a speed of 27 knots. She was, in effect, a fast battleship, superior to any comparable ship in British service, and she was a profound embarrassment to the British who built her. But *Kongo* was also the last capital ship built for Japan by a foreign power. Using *Kongo* as a model, the Japanese went on to complete three sister-ships – *Hiei*, *Haruna* and *Kirishima* – in their own yards.

When war broke out in 1914, Japan loyally collaborated with her British ally in hunting for German surface raiders in the Pacific, but there could be no mistaking the single-mindedness with which Japan attacked the German colonies north of the Equator. After seizing Tsingtau and the Shantung peninsula, Japan had then served China with her notorious '21 Demands' (January 1915). China's acceptance gave Japan a virtual monopoly of future foreign intervention in China and, after news of the '21 Demands' broke, the pre-1914 image of 'plucky little Japan' was gone for ever. At the same time the Japanese battle fleet continued to grow, four more 14-inch gun battleships being followed by *Nagato* and *Mutsu*, the world's first 16-inch gun battleships. Their completion ensured that the US Navy, which had moved up to the 14-inch gun with *New York* and *Texas* (BBs. 34 and 35, laid down in 1911) would go on to produce its own classes of 16-inch gun battleships in emulation.

The United States had one obvious disadvantage compared with Japan. American naval construction had to be planned with one eye on the Atlantic and the leading European navies and one eye on the Pacific and Japan, and in effect build two battleships for every one built in Japan. To offset this, however, the Panama Canal had finally been opened in August 1914, making it easier to

Previous pages: Ships of Admiral Halsey's 3rd Fleet during the battle for the Philippines in December 1944. Task Group 38.3 returns to its advance base at Ulithi Atoll, in line-ahead led by the light carrier USS *Langley* (CVL. 27) and 'Essex' class fleet carrier USS *Ticonderoga* (CV.14).

adjust the balance between the Atlantic and Pacific fleets as required. In 1916, the last year of American neutrality, Congress authorized the construction of a huge new fleet of 16-inch gun battleships intended to ensure a 'two-ocean' comparability for the US Navy. The new program fell into two parts: four 'Colorados' authorized in 1916, and six 'South Dakotas' authorized in 1917. Only one of these, *Maryland* (BB.46) had been laid down by the end of the war, and none of the 'South Dakotas' was laid down before 1920. But by then it was already clear that a new naval building race was under way between the United States and Japan, no less financially crippling and dangerous to world peace than the pre-1914 contest between Britain and Germany had been.

Japan's reply to the American 1916 program had been the '8-8' Program of 1918: a total of eight battleships (four 14-inch and four 16-inch) and eight battle-cruisers of similar armament. News of the '8-8' Program confirmed the American decision to add a third element to the 1916 expansion program: six 16-inch gun battle-cruisers ('Lexingtons'), a type which the US Navy had hitherto avoided. Britain, which had planned extensive fleet reductions for the 1920s, was distractedly obliged to order a new class of super-battle-cruiser to keep pace. By the spring of 1921 another global warship-building race was under way.

This renewed outburst of battleship mania

had serious results for the planned composition of the American fleet. One of the most valuable fruits of the close Anglo-American naval relationship in the last 18 months of the war had been access to the unrivaled British expertise in building aircraft-carriers: 'custom-built' for the job with workshops and hangars below a long flight-deck left unimpeded by a compact 'island' superstructure offset to one side. The addition of four 38,000-ton aircraft-carriers to the March 1919 Estimates was intended to give the US Navy carrier parity at a stroke – and outright carrier superiority over the Japanese, who had one small carrier (*Hosho*) building. The new American carriers were intended to operate with the 'Lexington' class battle-cruisers – but it was only with the greatest reluctance that Congress voted funds for the 'South Dakotas' and 'Lexingtons' in the 1920-21 Estimates. The proposed four carriers were rejected outright on grounds of cost, the only concession being permission to convert the fleet collier *Jupiter* as an experimental carrier.

Jupiter was taken in hand for conversion ·in March 1920 at the Norfolk Navy Yard – most appropriately, for it was here that the burned-out hulk of *Merrimack* had been converted into the ironclad *Virginia* in 1861-62. She recommissioned as USS *Langley*, Carrier Number One (CV.1) in March 1922 – by which time the naval construction story had been completely changed. Thanks to a

The US Navy's first carrier was the USS *Langley* (CV.1), a flush-decked conversion from the fleet collier *Jupiter*. Here she is shown under way with her radio masts lowered, recovering aircraft in the 1920s. *Langley's* affectionate Fleet nickname (as with Britain's *Furious* of similar vintage) was 'The Covered Wagon'.

remarkable international exercise in arms limitations, the battleship building race was over – at least for the foreseeable future.

This was the work of the Washington Naval Conference and Treaty (November 1921-February 1922), convened on the invitation of American President Warren Harding. The main items of agenda, from which there was no dissent, were that the situation in the Pacific and China needed definition by treaty and that the prospect of another international building race was intolerable. Separate treaties (with Japan agreeing to restore the Shantung peninsula to China) settled the political scene before the details of the naval agreement were hammered out. These proscribed the super-battleship as the world's most dangerous military status symbol, imposed restrictive limitations on future battleship tonnage and armament, and agreed on a ten-year 'holi-day' from new battleship construction. The tonnage and armament restrictions were an attempt to scotch battleship development by imposing what were then believed to be irreconcilable specifications: 35,000 tons maximum displacement and 16-inch maximum caliber for main armament.

The Washington Treaty also sought to make future building races among the signatory powers impossible, by assigning maximum permitted tonnage totals on a ratio basis: Britain 5, United States 5, Japan 3, France and Italy 1.67. Here was a special landmark in the history of the US Navy: the official grant of battleship parity between the British and American fleets. But the Treaty's most celebrated ploy was to tolerate new aircraft-carrier construction as a way of 'recycling' the battleship and battle-cruiser hulls already being built when the Washington Conference met. The carrier's maximum tonnage was set at 27,000 tons and its gun armament limited to a battery of no more than 10 guns with a maximum caliber of eight inches. But the naval powers at present locked into the battleship building race – the United States, Japan and latterly Britain – were given the option of converting two of their uncompleted hulls into heavy carriers of no more than 33,000 tons. For the rest, future carrier-building tonnage was allocated by ratio: Britain 5, United States 5, Japan 3, France and Italy 2.2. This worked out at 135,000 tons of carriers for Britain and the United States, 81,000 tons to Japan and

With the US Battle Fleet in March 1926, probably in Cuban waters. Identifiable are two battleships of the 'New Mexico' class and four destroyers – *Lavalette* (DD.315), *Wood* (DD.317), *Kidder* (DD.319) and *Chase* (DD.323) – all from the Battle Fleet; and one destroyer from the Scouting Fleet. Also present are an 'Omaha' class cruiser, an oiler, and other destroyers.

60,000 tons to France and Italy.

The trouble was that few in early 1922 had any clear idea what the carrier's true role should be. In general it was vaguely assumed to be an extension of the cruiser's traditional scouting role, with the carrier's gun armament envisaged for defense as much against surface as against air attack. There was virtually no notion of using carriers as a separate striking task force, with the battleships of the fleet offering heavy-gun support against enemy surface attack. Such thinking on tactics as existed saw the carrier's fleet role as primary reconnaissance, making the battleships' job easier – with the useful facility of being able to launch air attacks on enemy ships sheltering behind minefields or in anchorages too remote to be bombarded by an offshore battle fleet.

The first-fruit of the Washington Naval Treaty was the birth of the heavy fleet carrier: the US Navy's *Lexington* and *Saratoga,* Japan's *Kaga* and *Akagi,* all four converted from Treaty-banned capital ship hulls. All four, entering service in the later 1920s, demonstrated the Washington Treaty's gravest flaw: that there was no way of enforcing the Treaty's restrictions short of war, the avoidance of which was the Treaty's ultimate objective. All four of the heavy carriers were way over the specially-expanded limit of 33,000 tons permitted for these conversions, but both the US Navy and Japan 'bent the rules' in concocting acceptable figures. This process needed very little extension to become an easy way in which to flout the Treaty restrictions without calling down international censure. By the time of the London Naval Conference of 1930, which sought with considerably less success to extend the naval 'holiday,' there were already signs (most notably the increasing truculence of Japan) that the Washington Treaty's most solid achievements were short-term and impossible to repeat.

Meanwhile, the heavy-carrier conversions were put to work in fleet exercises which showed considerable promise for carrier task

The battleship USS *New York* (BB.34) leads USS *Nevada* (BB.36) and USS *Oklahoma* (BB.37) during Fleet exercises in 1932. On the horizon can be seen the unmistakable silhouette of the carrier USS *Langley*.

At the time of Pearl Harbor in December 1941 the US Navy had 112 submarines in commission with another 65 completed. These are all of the 'New "S"' class, launched in 1937-38: USS *Stingray* (SS.186), *Sturgeon* (SS.187), *Salmon* (SS.182) and *Seal* (SS.183), exercising with the Battle Force in 1939. All four survived the Second World War.

groups operating independently of the main battle fleet. The big question for the US Navy was whether its remaining allocated carrier tonnage should be taken up with a few more large carriers, or several smaller ones. The disappointing performance of the lightweight *Ranger* (launched in 1933) tipped the scale in favor of larger carriers (*Yorktown* and *Enterprise*, launched in 1936). After one last experiment with the light-carrier format with *Wasp* (launched in 1939) the carrier type chosen for the US Navy was the 'medium-heavy', 27,000-ton 'Essex' class, the first of which were ordered in the 1940 Construction Program. But none of the 'Essex' class carriers was ready for service before Japan attacked the United States in December 1941. Nor were the first of the fast 16-inch gun battleships ('North Carolina' and 'South Dakota' classes) ordered in the 1937 and 1938 Programs. Ironically, these new battleships solved the problem of getting a full battery of 16-inch guns into 35,000 tons displacement (by using triple instead of twin turret mountings) long after the Washington Treaty was dead in spirit as well as in letter.

In its two years and three months of wartime neutrality before Pearl Harbor, the US Navy benefited enormously from British wartime experience in the Narrow Seas, Atlantic, Arctic and Mediterranean. The two most obvious of these British-inspired benefits were sonar, for detecting submerged submarines, and radar for surface and air surveillance, invented by the British and perfected by American technology. The British also served as guinea-pigs in the hitherto unknown field of how modern warships would stand up to expert air attack, showing that no anti-aircraft battery of rapid-firing guns could really be considered sufficient. The loss of the British carrier *Courageous* in September 1939 and of *Glorious* in June 1940, respectively to U-boat and surface attack, showed the supreme vulnerability of carriers when exposed without adequate anti-submarine screening or heavy ship support. Finally, the British search for auxiliary air cover which could be extended to cover convoys produced the new concept of the escort carrier, converted from merchant ships. When mass-produced by American shipyards with their world-beating capacity, escort carriers became the means by which the fleet carriers were completely freed for purely offensive instead of supportive operations. *Long Island*, the US Navy's first escort carrier (CVE), was completed over six months before Pearl Harbor, at the beginning of June 1941.

Setting aside these crucial debts to British technology and combat experience, in the renewal of basic warship types the US Navy had been far better served than the Royal Navy during the 1930s. (Having a 'Navy-minded' President in Franklin D. Roosevelt, who as a rising young politician had served as Assistant Navy Secretary, was an invaluable boon.) In the seven years between Roosevelt's first inauguration as President in 1933 and the outbreak of the European war in September 1939, successive Construction Programs ordered a total of four aircraft-carriers, six battleships, three heavy cruisers, 13 light cruisers, 83 destroyers and 38 submarines. But the emergency 1940 Program – cast in the light of the German bid for mastery in Europe – alone ordered nine battleships, 17 carriers, eight heavy cruisers, 38 light cruisers, 196 destroyers and 73 submarines. This was virtually *double* the *combined total* of the Programs *for the previous seven years*, most of whose ships were completed in time to help bear the brunt of

the Japanese offensive in 1941-42. The new ships coming forward in the last five years of peace before Pearl Harbor were ample to replace those lost in the US Navy's first year of war: two battleships, four carriers, five heavy cruisers, two light cruisers, 27 destroyers and eight submarines.

The assurance of ample warship replacements, however, only spelled comfort for the future; they could do nothing to halt the

Above: Fine shot of the Battle Force at sea in 1939. It was not until the Pacific Fleet's battle line was liquidated at Pearl Harbor that the new carrier arm became the US Navy's dominant arm.

The cruiser USS *Phoenix* (CVL.46) passes the funeral pyre of the battle line at Pearl Harbor.
Inset: USS *Nevada* (compare with pp. 104-105), beached and burning after failing to escape to the open sea during the Japanese attack.

be spared from the Atlantic, where the battle against Germany's U-boats was necessarily left to the hard-pressed Royal Navy in 1942. In the Pacific, therefore, the traditional concept of an American battle fleet supported by carriers was shattered for ever by the Pearl Harbor disaster. Only a handful of American carriers and cruisers remained, apparently the flimsiest of weapons with which to oppose the Japanese Combined Fleet at the peak of its strength.

Yet they were just enough. Within six months of Pearl Harbor, two major Japanese offensives had been frustrated by carrier battles in which, for the first time, neither fleet ever sighted the other. And in these battles – the Coral Sea (May 1942) and Midway (June 1942) – the Japanese superiority in carriers was wiped out. For this reversal, Japanese over-confidence and un-

realistic planning played a major part. But there can be no detracting from the US Navy's achievement against all odds, for which five American admirals claim an enduring share of fame.

Ernest J. King (1878-1956) was the man at the top, directly under Roosevelt as Commander-in-Chief of the US Armed Forces. In the inevitable command changes after Pearl Harbor, King was advanced from C-in-C

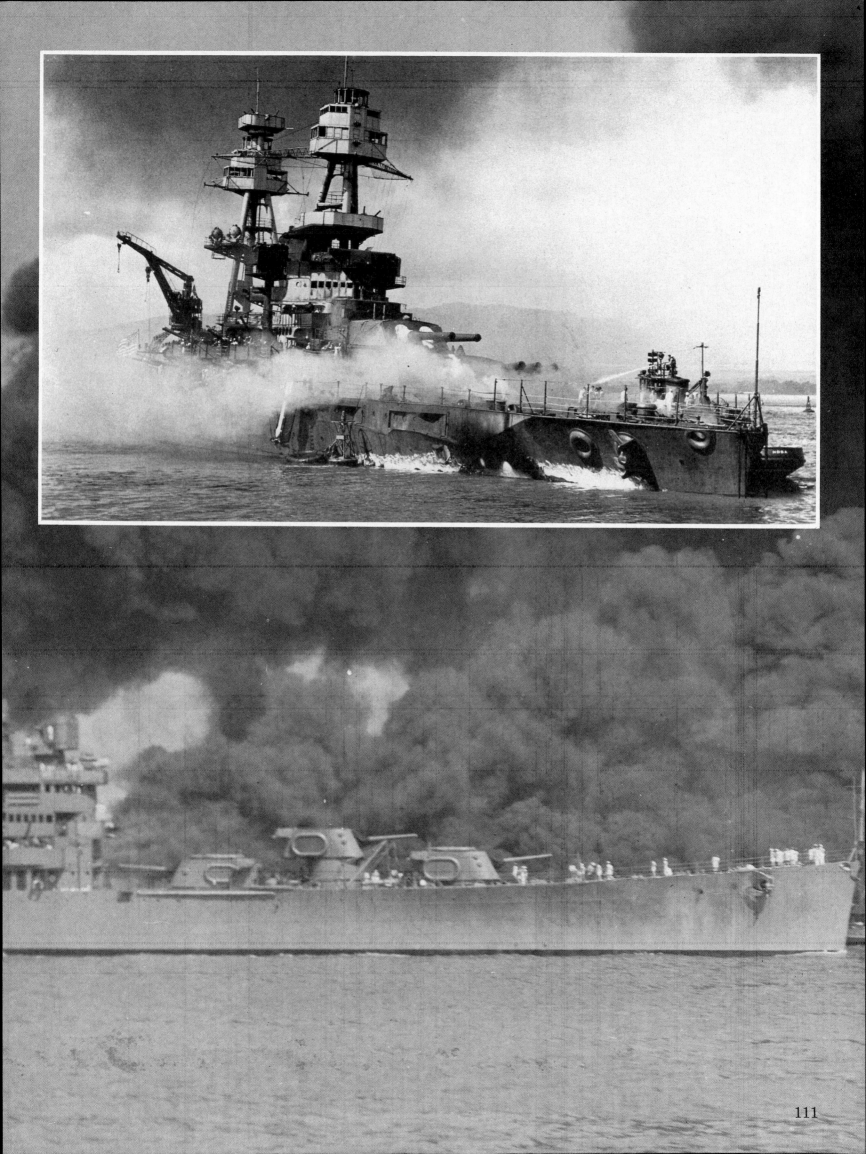

Atlantic Fleet (CINCLANT) to Commander-in-Chief, US Fleet (COMUNCH). A hardcore professional who never lost faith that the US Navy would come through to win the war, King's greatest achievement was in picking the man who would start the job by restoring faith and fighting efficiency to the US Pacific Fleet: Admiral Chester W. Nimitz (1885-1966).

Patient, shrewd, with all the warmer human qualities lacking in the more forbidding character of King, Nimitz had the gift of extracting the maximum results from the minimum resources – human and *materiel*. He was the ideal commander to take up King's brief in December 1941: 'Hold what you've got and hit them where you can.' Few commanders ever showed more skill in exploiting that most unpredictable of factors in war: the enemy's mistakes.

The gutsy and ebullient William F. Halsey (1882-1959) embodied the fighting spirit of the US carrier arm, with his slogans, 'Before we've finished with 'em, the Japanese language will be spoken only in hell!' and 'Kill Japs, kill Japs, kill more Japs!' He commanded the carrier raid which on 18 April 1942 launched Army B-25s to bomb Tokyo – the most convincing proof possible that the US Pacific Fleet was still a force to be reckoned with. The Tokyo Raid deprived Halsey of the chance of joining the fray in the Coral Sea battle (4-8 May 1942), which foiled the Japanese conquest of Port Moresby and saved a vital foothold in New Guinea for the

Right: USS *Enterprise* (CV.6) recovering Dauntless strike aircraft off Guadalcanal in December 1942, with USS *Saratoga* (CV.3) in background. Three other aircraft can be seen above the tailfin of the Dauntless in foreground.
Below: A Hellcat of VF-1 'Top Hat' Squadron, poised for take-off from the second *Yorktown* (CV.10) during the 'Great Marianas Turkey Shoot' in June 1944.

Allies. When sickness forced Halsey ashore on the eve of the supreme trial at Midway, his choice of successor proved to be one of the greatest naval tacticians of the new carrier era.

Frank Jack Fletcher (1885-1973) was, with Halsey, the foremost carrier task force commander in the hit-and-run raids on the Japanese perimeter, ordered by Nimitz in the spring of 1942. Fletcher won the Battle of the Coral Sea and, until his flagship *Yorktown* was mortally damaged, commanded the US carrier ambush on the Japanese at Midway on 4 June 1942. Thus deprived of effective command with the Midway battle still hanging in the balance, Fletcher wisely decided to conform to the movements of Halsey's chosen successor, Raymond A. Spruance (1886-1969), who until Halsey's illness had commanded the cruiser element in Halsey's task Force. Thanks to the combined judgment of Fletcher and Spruance and the supreme gallantry of the aircrews of *Yorktown, Enterprise* and *Hornet*, four of the six Japanese carriers which had struck at Pearl Harbor were sunk and carrier parity between the American and Japanese navies precariously restored.

After Midway came the long agony of Guadalcanal (August 1942-February 1943): a merciless battle of attrition in the central Solomon Islands, with both navies at full stretch to supply their troops locked in combat on Guadalcanal. The campaign was fought to the limit of endurance, with two more daytime carrier battles (Eastern Solomons on 24 August and Santa Cruz on 26 October), and a string of vicious night actions between the rival cruiser/destroyer forces. By November 1942 the US Pacific Fleet was down to its last operational carrier, *Enterprise. Wasp* and *Hornet* had followed *Yorktown* (lost at Midway) and *Lexington* (lost at the Coral Sea). Both sides finally committed battleships to the Guadalcanal night fighting, with the new American *Washington* and *South Dakota* finally tipping the balance on the night of 14-15 November 1942. From then on the Japanese were reduced to supplying their army on Guadalcanal with clandestine night runs, having lost the equivalent of an entire peacetime fleet since the

Previous pages: Hellcat fighters (foreground) and Avenger strike aircraft ranged for take-off on a US carrier.
Left: The first two US fleet carriers lost in the Pacific War were USS *Lexington* (CV.2) at Coral Sea in May 1942, and *(below)* the first *Yorktown* (CV.5) at Midway in June 1942. By the end of the year *Wasp* and *Hornet* had followed, both sunk off Guadalcanal; with *Saratoga* damaged, this briefly left *Enterprise* as the only operational US fleet carrier in the Pacific.

117

The battleship *New Mexico* (BB.40) added fire power to every major US Pacific amphibious operation, from the recapture of the western Aleutians in 1943 to Okinawa in 1945.

Right: The two forward turrets of the main battery: 14-inch guns in triple mountings. *Opposite:* The heavy guns of the vital anti-aircraft umbrella – 5-inch AA guns at exercise.

Above: Devastator torpedo-bombers prepare for launch from *Enterprise* during the Battle of Midway (June 1942). Bereft of close fighter cover, slow and vulnerable, only four of the aircraft in this picture came back.

on the ground had conquered enough real estate for land-based air cover to take over. The inevitable result was to deprive the US carriers of their most valuable asset – operating from 'no fixed address' – thus exposing them to heavy losses from Japanese submarine and carrier attack. The victory was another triumph for Nimitz, who refused to despair when American prospects seemed darkest; and for Halsey, appointed by Nimitz as Commander-in-Chief, South Pacific (ComSoPac).

After Guadalcanal, Halsey remained as ComSoPac to direct the dogged advance up the Solomons chain which culminated in the invasion of Bougainville on 31 October 1943. Spruance was meanwhile appointed by Nimitz to command the 5th Fleet: the ever-increasing concentration of new carriers ('Essex' and 'Independence' classes) which arrived in the Pacific from the autumn of 1943. Backed by an armada of storeships and tankers to remain at sea for weeks on end, withdrawing between attacks to advance bases created from empty coral atolls, the 5th Fleet launched the long-awaited break-in to the Central Pacific with its attack on the Gilberts in November 1943. The Marshalls followed in February 1944 and then on 16 June 1944 the 5th Fleet covered the invasion of Saipan in the Marianas, which brought on the last great carrier battle of the Pacific War: the Battle of the Philippine Sea (19-20

start of the campaign: two battleships, one carrier, five cruisers, 12 destroyers and eight submarines. When this last desperate venture failed, the Japanese High Command accepted the inevitable and ordered the evacuation of Guadalcanal.

The Guadalcanal victory was an extraordinary achievement by the US Navy. The campaign was fought and won on two levels: the Navy's determination not to leave the Marine garrison to its fate, and the attempt to maintain naval air cover until the troops

June 1944).

The Philippine Sea was Spruance's greatest tactical triumph, in which he refused to expose the Saipan invasion fleet and waited for the Japanese to come to him – to be shot down in scores by the 5th Fleet's carrier fighters. It was the swansong of the Japanese carrier arm, which went into battle with 430 aircraft against 891 and came out with only 35 – the 'Great Marianas Turkey Shoot,' as the Americans exultingly dubbed the engagement. After the Philippine Sea, the last operational Japanese carriers were toothless tigers, useful only as decoys in the extraordinary plan concocted for the defense of the Philippines: 'Sho-Go'.

Above: Top brass on Saipan – the leading UD admirals of the Second World War, with Fleet Admiral 'Ernie' King (COMINCH) at center.

Below: Enterprise at speed during the Battle of Midway, with a cruiser of the screen at right of picture.

6: SHIELD OF THE FREE WORLD 1945-1984

Mothballed American destroyers, all capable of speedy return to front-line service, on the Pacific coast in July 1966. Preserving obsolescent ships instead of scrapping them has always been a prudent hallmark of the US Navy.

The guided missile frigate USS *Oliver Hazard Perry* (FFG.7), commissioned in December 1977. She carries 40 Harpoon/Standard surface/AA missiles, two helicopters in the after hangar, a 76mm gun, and two triple torpedo tubes for anti-submarine work – all-round potential in a hull displacing 3,605 tons (3,663 tonnes) at full load.

Above: A US Navy F-4B Phantom in a high-level bombing attack over Vietnam.

Right: The battleship USS *New Jersey* (BB.62) firing her full 16-inch broadside during her 1968-69 recommission for service in the Vietnam War.

USS *Long Beach* (CGN.9) was the first American cruiser designed since 1941; the world's first nuclear-powered surface warship; and the first surface warship armed with a guided-missile main battery. She was brought into service in September 1961.

June 1982: USS *Ticonderoga*, first ship of the newest American class of guided-missile cruisers, armed with the Aegis missile system, underway in the Gulf of Mexico.

The Combat Information Center (CIC) in USS *Ticonderoga*. Here are displayed the data gathered by the ship's four fixed-array AN/SPY 1A radars, revealing situations which might threaten the ship and the battle group she is designed to protect. The ship's weapons – AA and surface missiles, rapid-firing deck guns, anti-submarine torpedoes and rockets – are all directed and fired from the CIC.

pared with only 771 between 1943 and 1945) during her experimental recommission in 1968-69. It was calculated that the $21 million cost of her refit and recommission was equal to the value of six shot-down F4 Phantom aircraft. Within another ten years the heartfelt advocacy of former pilots was pressing for yet another return of *New Jersey* to active service, this time as a combined missile and big-gun platform. In this new guise her awesome silhouette appeared off the strife-torn coast of Beirut in the New Year of 1984, supporting the 6th Fleet's abortive 'peace-keeping' mission, hurling 16-inch shells across the Shouf Moutains onto rebel PLO gun positions.

Extending the operational careers of veter-

an warships past all known limits has gone hand in hand with a formidable inventiveness in new technologies and new ship types. This has been most obvious in the two mainstays of American sea power since 1945: the giant carrier and the submarine.

The big carrier was the natural legacy of the Pacific War in which, after 1942, the only American carriers lost were the lightweight 'Independence' class *Princeton* and five escort carriers. From this experience, American carrier doctrine argues that a big carrier stands a better chance of surviving submarine or air attack, and can also mount more anti-aircraft guns (or, latterly, missiles). More obviously, the bigger the carrier, the bigger (and better balanced) the air group can be. This means more fighters both for defense from air attacks, and for escorting attack missions flown by the carrier's strike aircraft. Big carriers also proved perfectly suited to operating the new jet aircraft of the postwar era, with their increased deadweights and flying speeds. The first jet-powered carrier launch (of a McDonnell FH-1 Phantom) was made from *Coral Sea* in July 1946.

After a false start with *United States* (aborted in 1949) American heavy-carrier development was resumed in the light of

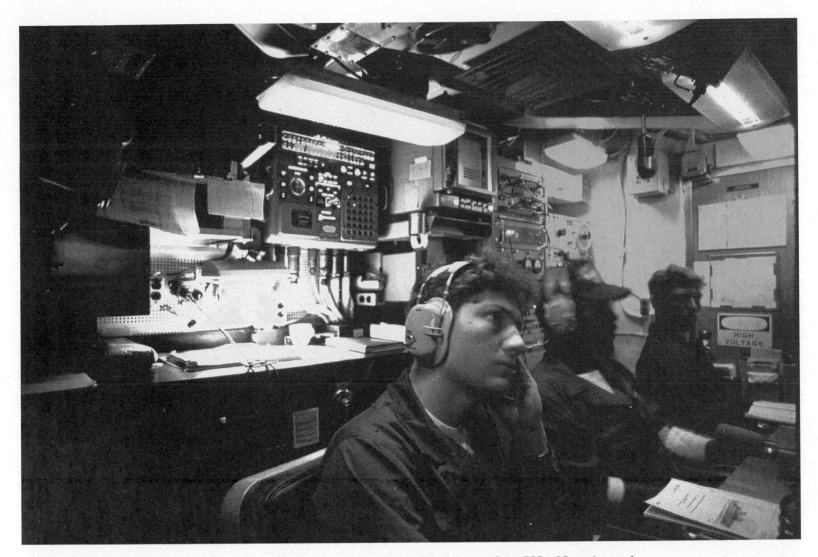

Sonar Technicians man their underwater watch stations at the console aboard the 'Los Angeles' class nuclear-powered attack submarine USS *La Jolla*.

Korean War experience. The result was the four-ship 'Forrestal' class (*Forrestal, Saratoga, Ranger,* and *Independence*), the first of which was ordered in 1952. These mighty ships, with their full-displacement of 78,000 tons, were the first post-1945 heavy carriers, designed and built specifically for operating jet aircraft. They gave the US Navy an entirely new strategic function: as a global vehicle for the American nuclear deterrent. Though the simultaneous development of the ballistic missile-firing submarine (SSBN) soon robbed the American carrier arm of a monopoly in nuclear 'clout', the Forrestals served as prototypes for the mightiest floating structures ever built by man: the nuclear-powered *Enterprise* which was commissioned in 1961 and ultimately the 91,500-ton *Nimitz* (commissioned 1975) and her successors.

Not content with transforming the role of the heavy fleet carrier, the US Navy was simultaneously achieving the same for its submarine arm. The end of the Pacific War had carried the American submarine arm to an unprecedented eminence. In the submarine 'Battle of the Pacific' against Japanese shipping, the US Navy's submarines – though only amounting to two percent of the total American naval strength in the Pacific, destroyed 61 percent of the Japanese merchant fleet. The ravages caused by the American submarines made it impossible for the Japanese to ship troops and supplies to the island garrisons menaced by the US carrier task forces, completely distrupted the internal sealanes of the Japanese Empire, and were a major factor in bringing about the early end of the war. They succeeded, in short, where Germany's U-boats had failed in the Atlantic, and the significance of this was not forgotten after the Japanese defeat.

American submarine development after 1945 was aimed at pushing the conventional diesel/electric submarine to the limit and to developing a practicable nuclear power plant. The first stage was perfecting a streamlined hull which would yield high submerged speeds. The now-familiar 'teardrop' or 'whale' shape was proven by the experimental *Albacore* (1953), the first submarine to break 30 knots when submerged. The first nuclear-powered submarines,

Stunning head-on shot of the 'super-carrier' USS *Carl Vinson* (CVN.70), third ship of the nuclear-powered 'Nimitz' class. With a deep-load displacement of 91,487 tons (92,951 tonnes), these carriers are the biggest warships of all time.

Poised for launch from the steam catapult: a Grumman F-14 Tomcat. This advanced 'swing-wing' all-weather fighter (the wings retract aft for high-speed flight) has a maximum speed of Mach 2.4.

USS *Enterprise*, the US Navy's first nuclear-powered 'super-carrier'. When completed in 1961 she was the largest floating structure ever built by man, but still took only 31 months from laying-down to launch.

7:THE U.S. NAVY TODAY

The US Navy is the largest and most powerful navy the world has yet seen, possessing truly global capability for the protection for the USA and its interests, and for the projection of American power. The three principal components of the US Navy are its submarine arm, heavily biased in favour of nuclear-powered boats; its maritime air arm, centred on multi-role aircraft-carriers carrying a diversity of offensive/ defensive aircraft and protected by missile-armed cruisers and destroyers; and its amphibious arm, dedicated to the carriage and shoreward delivery of the US Marine Corps, and usually protected by frigates. The submarine arm is being rationalised at the moment, with heavy emphasis on the rapid construction of the 'Ohio' class SSBN and 'Los Angeles' class SSN to allow the retirement of older classes. The SSBN's are being equipped with the Trident I C4 strategic missiles as a replacement for the older Poseidon C3, and will soon begin to receive the definitive Trident II D5; combined with improved communications capability for submerged submarines (thanks to the development of ELF and new TACAMO systems), greater reliance can be placed on the rapid and accurate response capabilities of the SSBN force, helping to promote it towards the primary position amongst the elements of the US offensive strategic triad (land-based missiles, air-released bombs and missiles and submarine-launched missiles). The SSN force is designed for two offensive/ defensive functions, namely the defence of the USA by attacks on Soviet missile-carrying submarines, and the defence of carrier task groups by attacks on Soviet submarines equipped with torpedoes (of which about half are nuclear-tipped). But while in theory the concentration on the 'Ohio' and 'Los Angeles' classes is excellent, offering the possibility of large standardized forces, the programme has run into immense problems of cost escalation and production slippages, requiring the retention of older vessels as a stopgap. Moreover, while the capability of the new classes is unquestionable, so too is their vulnerability, for both classes are extremely large and relatively noisy. And the very size of the 'Los Angeles' class raises another problem, for it makes it difficult for the boats of the class to operate in the shallow waters of the large continental shelf areas, where Soviet boats could well lurk for some time. It would seem sensible, therefore, for the US Navy to develop a new class of diesel-electric hunter-killer submarine for this specific purpose, but so entrenched is the position of the nuclear-boat lobby that this seems impossibly difficult to achieve.

Naval aviation in the US Navy rests with the aircraft-carrier force, planned at 15 carrier air wings (one per carrier) but currently operational as only 12 carrier air wings. This is still a formidable capability, given that each carrier air wing can muster up to 80 or more aircraft (usually two fighter squadrons, one medium attack squadron, one light attack squadron and two anti-submarine squadrons, plus support aircraft) of the US Navy and US Marine Corps, but leaves the US Navy with little reserve capacity. Four more of the massive nuclear-powered 'Nimitz' class carriers are planned or building, which will improve matters considerably, but in the short term the deficiency is being made good in an alternative fashion by the reactivation and modernization (with missiles and modern sensors) of two (possibly four) 'Iowa' class battleships. Though these cannot carry the aircraft of a carrier air wing (though a complement of V/STOL strike aircraft is planned when the ships are modernised yet further), they do have formidable gun and missile firepower.

Escort of each carrier task group is theoretically entrusted to two missile-armed cruisers (nuclear-powered in groups which are centred on a nuclear carrier) plus a number of missile-armed destroyers. A shortfall in numbers has often meant, however, that frigates have to be included in the escort force as part of the outer screen. The situation should be improved greatly with the delivery of additional 'Ticonderoga' class cruisers, with their highly capable AEGIS analysis and control functions, and with the first arrivals of the 'Arleigh Burke' class destroyers at the end of the decade. Hand-in-hand with this ship and sensor modification programme goes a constant upgrading of the vital Standard missile, designed principally as an air-defence weapon but possessing a limited anti-ship capability and being developed into a longer-range and more accurate weapon system. Other missile developments centre on the widespread deployment of the medium-range Harpoon anti-ship missile, and the installation on larger ships of the Tomahawk cruise missile for long-range anti-ship defence. Close-range air-defence remains a problem, the Sea Sparrow system being too slow in launch, and the Phalanx 20-mm CIWS mounting lacking sufficient punch for last-ditch defence against sea-skimming anti-ship missiles. It is anticipated that the capability and versatility of ship-board missile systems will be much enhanced later in the decade by the adoption of vertical-launch systems capable of handling anti-ship, anti-aircraft and anti-submarine missiles of several types.

Amphibious forces are in something of a quandary at the moment, for the precise role of the US Marine Corps remains uncertain. Amphibious operations are clearly important, but their precise nature (and perhaps their vulnerability) remains open to question. Nevertheless their ships are being developed and built as a matter of urgency as the need to replace older units becomes more apparent. One of the problems is that these large and lightly defended targets require extensive escort protection from frigates armed with anti-ship and anti-aircraft missiles, and that the frigates are in short supply because of the need for their deployment in carrier task group escort forces.

The US Navy has an all-volunteer personnel strength, this amounting at the moment to some 569,000 including 42,700 women. Naval air-power, which has about 1,450 combat aircraft and 160 combat helicopters, is included in this total, and operates 24 fighter squadrons, 12 medium attack squadrons, 24 light attack squadrons, 11 shipboard anti-submarine squadrons, 11 fixed- and 17 rotary-wing anti-submarine squadrons, 12 airborne early warning squadrons, 24 land-based maritime reconnaissance and anti-submarine squadrons, two mine countermeasures helicopter squadrons, 22 operational conversion units, 18 training squadrons and 17 miscellaneous squadrons.

Operationally, the US Navy is divided into four fleets controlled by two command organizations: headquartered at Norfolk, Virginia, the Atlantic Fleet contols the 2nd Fleet (headquarters in Norfolk) and the 6th Fleet (headquarters at Gaeta in Italy) for operations in the Mediterranean; and headquartered at Pearl Harbour, Hawaii, the Pacific Fleet controls the 3rd Fleet (headquarters at Pearl Harbour) and the 7th Fleet (headquarters at Yokohama in Japan for operations in the western Pacific with detachments into the Indian Ocean and Persian Gulf areas). With other continental bases at Bangor, Boston, Brunswick, Charleston, Jacksonville, Kings Bay, New London, New Orleans and Newport, the 2nd Fleet has overseas bases at Guantanamo Bay (Cuba), Holy Loch (UK), Keflavik (Iceland) and Roosevelt Roads (Puerto Rico), and generally deploys 31 SSBNs, 41 SSNs, 76 surface combatants and 27 amphibious warfare vessels. Apart from its base at Gaeta, the 6th Fleet has a base at La Rota in Spain and at La Maddalena, Naples and Sigonella in Italy, and usually musters some two SSNs, one or two aircraft-carriers and about 38 other surface combatants and amphibious warfare vessels. The 3rd Fleet has additional bases at Adak, Long Beach, San Diego, San Francisco and Whidbey Island, and has a typical strength of two SSBNs, 30 SSNs, three carriers, one battleship and about 44 other surface combatants plus 31 amphibious warfare vessels. And the 7th Fleet, with additional bases at Agena and Apra Harbor on Guam, Midway Island, Subic Bay in the Philippines and forward facilities in the Indian Ocean at Diego Suarez, operates a few SSNs on temporary assignment, plus some 45 surface combatants including three or four carriers; the detachments in the Indian Ocean and Persian Gulf, often supported by vessels from the 6th Fleet, generally comprise a carrier task group with five escorts in the former, and two destroyers plus a command ship in the latter.

US Navy Reserves amount to an extra 87,900 men, and these man a varying number of ships, normally about three destroyers and six frigates, and also provide the manpower strength for two additional carrier air wings, two maritime reconnaissance wings and one tactical support wing (all with fixed-wing aircraft), plus one helicopter wing.

The US Coast Guard service is administered by the Department of Transportation, but in war comes under the operational control of the US Navy as part of the armed forces. Regular strength is 38,800 including 1,800 women, and there are 11,800 reservists. Ship assets comprise 17 high-endurance cutters (small destroyers), 28 medium-endurance cutters (lightweight frigates), six icebreakers, 76 patrol craft, and 118 other craft. The US Coast Guard also possesses a small air arm with 41 fixed- and rotary-wing aircraft, most of them dedicated to patrol and search-and-rescue.

USN ship strength

type	class	number
SUBMARINES		
strategic,	'Ohio'	8 (+6 ordered)
ballistic-missile,	'Benjamin Franklin'	12
nuclear-powered	'James Madison'	8
	'Lafayette'	8
fleet attack	'Los Angeles'	36
nuclear-powered	'Sturgeon'	35
(SSN)		
	'Permit'	
	(ex 'Thresher')	13
	'Glenard P. Lipscomb'	1
	'Narwhal'	1
	'Skipjack'	4 (3 in 87/88)
	'Skate'	2 (1 in 87/88)
attack, diesel-powered	'Barbel'	2
(SS)	'Darter'	1
SSNs, other roles		
Deep SAR	'Sturgeon'	2
SF transport	'Ethan Allen'	2
transport	'Tullibee'	1
AIRCRAFT CARRIERS		
nuclear (CVN)	'Nimitz'	4
	'Enterprise'	1
conventional (CV)	'Kitty Hawk'	3
	'John F. Kennedy'	1
	'Forrestal'	4
	'Midway'	2
BATTLESHIP (BBG)	'Iowa'	3 (+1 refit)
CRUISERS		
nuclear-powered	'Virginia'	4
(CGN)	'California'	2
	'Truxton'	1
	'Long Beach'	1
	'Bainbridge'	1
conventionally-	'Ticonderoga'	9
powered (CG)	'Belknap'	9
	'Leahy'	9
DESTROYERS		
guided missile	'Kidd'	4
(DDG)	'Coontz'	10
	'Charles F. Adams'	23
anti-submarine (DD)	'Spruance'	31
FRIGATES		
guided missile	'Oliver Hazard Perry'	50
(FFG)	'Brook'	6
gun/ASW	'Knox'	46
	Garcia'	10
	'Glover'	1
	'Bronstein'	2
AMPHIBIOUS OPERATIONS		
command (LCC)	'Blue Ridge'	2
assault (LHA)	'Tarawa'	5
assault (LPH)	'Iwo Jima'	7
assault (LPD)	'Austin'	11
	'Raleigh'	2
assault (LSD)	'Whidbey'	2
	'Anchorage'	5
	'Thomaston'	3
(LST)	'Newport'	18
cargo (LKA)	'Charleston'	5
landing craft	Air cushion (LCAC)	9 (+27 ordered)
	Utility: Type 1610	53
	Type 1466	4
patrol craft		
hydrofoil (PHM)	'Pegasus'	6
inshore & river		
(PB, PCF, PBR)		85
MINESWEEPERS		
ocean	'Aggressive'	3
inshore boats (MSB)		7

Figures do not include Active Auxiliary Ships: 84; Military Sealift Command: 123; Ready Reserve Force: 85; National Defense Reserve Fleet: 176; Ships on Inactive Reserve/Storage: 46.

IOWA CLASS BATTLESHIP

CALIFORNIA CLASS NUCLEAR-POWERED GUIDED MISSILE CRUISER

TICONDEROGA CLASS GUIDED MISSILE CRUISER

TRUXTON CLASS NUCLEAR-POWERED GUIDED MISSILE CRUISER

Displacement: 45,000 tons standard and 58,000 tons full load
Dimensions: length 270.4m (887.2ft); beam 33.0m (108.2ft); draught 11.6m (38ft)
Gun Armament: Nine 406mm (16in) L/50 in three triple mountings, 12 127mm (5in) L/38 DP in six Mk 38 twin mountings, and four 20mm (0.8in) Phalanx Mk 15 close-in weapon system mountings
Missile Armament: Eight quadruple launchers for 32 BGM–109 Tomahawk cruise missiles, and four launchers for 16 RGM-84A Harpoon surface-to-surface missiles
Anti-submarine Armament: Helicopter-launched weapons
Aircraft: Three or four helicopters on a platform aft

Armour: 343/41mm (13.5/1.62in) belt, 152mm (6in) decks, 432/184mm (17/7.25in) turrets, 439mm (17.3in) barbettes, and 445/184mm (17.5/7.25in) conning tower
Propulsion: Eight Babcock & Wilcox boilers supplying steam to four sets of geared turbines (General Electric in BBs 61 and 63, Westinghouse in BBs 62 and 64) delivering 158,090kW (212,00shp) to four shafts
Performance: Maximum speed 33kts; range 27,800km (17,275mls) at 17kts
Complement: 1,571

Displacement: 9,560 tons standard and 11,100 tons full load
Dimensions: length 181.7m (596ft); beam 18.6m (61ft); draught 9.6m (31.5ft)
Gun Armament: Two 127mm (5in) L/54 DP in two Mk 42 single mountings, and (to be fitted) two Phalanx Mk 15 20mm (0.8in) close-in weapons system mountings
Missile Armament: Two quadruple container-launchers for eight BGM–109 Tomahawk surface-to-surface missiles, two quadruple launchers for eight RGM-84A Harpoon surface-to-surface missiles, and two Mk 13 single launchers for 80 RIM-66C Standard MR surface-to-air missiles
Anti-submarine Armament: One octuple Mk 16 launcher for RUR-5A ASROC missiles, and two triple Mk 32 tube mountings for 324mm (12.75in) Mk 46 A/S torpedoes

Propulsion: Two General Electric D2G pressurized-water cooled reactors supplying steam to two geared turbines delivering 44,740kW (60,000shp) to two shafts
Performance: Maximum speed 30kts; nuclear core life about 1,126,500km (700,000mls)
Complement: 28+512

Displacement: 9,600 tons full load
Dimensions: length 172.8m (566.8ft); beam 16.8m (55ft); draught 9.5m (31ft)
Gun Armament: Two 127mm (5in) L/54 DP in two Mk 45 single mountings, and two 20mm (0.79in) Phalanx Mk 15 close-in weapon system mountings
Missile Armament: Two octuple container-launchers for 16 RGM-84A Harpoon surface-to-surface missiles, and two Mk 26 twin launchers for up to 68 RIM–67B Standard surface-to-air missiles; from CG49 onwards the ships will have two EX 41 vertical launchers in place of the Mk 26 launchers for up to 122 assorted missiles, and from CG 52 onwards the ships will have two Vertical Launch Systems each with 12 BGM–109 Tomahawk surface-to-surface cruise missiles

Anti-submarine Armament: Two triple Mk 32 tube mountings for 324mm (12.75in) Mk 46 A/S torpedos, up to 20 RUR-5A ASROC missiles forming part of the total missile strength above and launched from the Mk 26 launchers, and helicopter-launched weapons
Aircraft: Two Sikorsky SH-60B Seahawk helicopters
Propulsion: Four General Electric LM 2500 gas turbines delivering 59,655kW (80,000shp) to two shafts
Performance: Maximum speed 30+kts
Complement: 33+327

Displacement: 8,200 tons standard and 9,125 tons full load
Dimensions: length 171.9m (564ft); beam 17.7m (58ft); draught 9.4m (31ft)
Gun Armament: One 127mm (5in) L/54 DP in one Mk 24 single mounting and two 20mm (0.79in) Phalanx Mk 15 close-in weapon system mountings
Missile Armament: Two quadruple container-launchers for eight RGM–84A Harpoon surface-to-surface missiles, and one Mk 10 twin launcher for up to 60 RIM–67B Standard-ER surface-to-air missiles
Anti-submarine Armament: Four Mk 32 tubes for 324mm (12.75in) Mk 46 A/S torpedoes, up to 20 RUR-5A ASROC missiles included in the total above for the Mk 10 launcher and launched from the Mk 10 launcher, and helicopter-launched weapons
Aircraft: One Kaman SH-2F Seasprite helicopter

Propulsion: Two pressurized-water cooled General Electric O2G nuclear reactors supplying steam to two sets of geared turbines delivering 44,740kW (60,000shp) to two shafts
Performance: Maximum speed 38kts
Complement: 36+492, plus flag accommodation for 6

ENTERPRISE CLASS NUCLEAR-POWERED
MULTI-ROLE AIRCRAFT CARRIER

FORRESTAL CLASS MULTI-ROLE AIRCRAFT CARRIER

JOHN F. KENNEDY CLASS MULTI-ROLE AIRCRAFT CARRIER

NIMITZ CLASS NUCLEAR-POWERED MULTI-ROLE AIRCRAFT-CARRIER

Displacement: 75,700 tons standard and 89,600 tons full load

Dimensions: length 335.9m (1,102ft); beam 40.5m (133ft); draught 10.9m (35.8ft); flight deck width 76.8m (252ft)

Gun Armament: Three Phalanx Mk 15 20mm (0.8in) close-in weapon systems, and three 20mm (0.8in) Mk 68 mountings

Missile Armament: Three Mk 57 launchers for RIM-7 NATO Sea Sparrow surface-to-air missiles

Aircraft: About 84

Propulsion: Eight pressurized-water cooled Westinghouse A2W reactors supplying steam to four sets of Westinghouse geared turbines delivering 208,795kW (280,000shp) to four shafts

Performance: Maximum speed 35kts; range 741,245km (460,600mls)

Complement: 162+2940, plus a carrier air-wing complement of 304+2,300

Displacement: 56,060 tons standard and 75,900 tons full load

Dimensions: length 331.0m (1,086ft); beam 39.5m (129.5ft); draught 11.3m (37ft); flight deck width 76.8m (252ft)

Gun Armament: To be fitted with three 20mm (0.8in) Phalanx Mk 16 close-in weapon system mountings

Missile Armament: Two Mk 25 octuple launchers for RIM-7 Sea Sparrow surface-to-air missiles

Aircraft: About 70

Propulsion: Eight Babcock & Wilcox boilers supplying steam to four sets of Westinghouse geared turbines delivering 193,880kW (260,000shp)

Performance: Maximum speed 33kts; range 14,805km (9,200mls) at 20kts or 7,400km (4,600mls) at 30kts

Complement: 145+2625, plus a carrier air-wing complement of about 2,130

Displacement: 61,000 tons standard and 82,000 tons full load

Dimensions: length 320.7m (1,052ft); beam 39.6m (130ft); draught 10.9m (35.9ft); flight deck width 76.9m (252ft)

Gun Armament: Three 20mm (0.8in) Phalanx Mk 15 close-in weapon system mountings

Missile Armament: Three Mk 29 launchers for RIM-7 Sea Sparrow surface-to-air missiles

Aircraft: About 85

Propulsion: Eight Foster-Wheeler boilers supplying steam to four sets of Westinghouse geared turbines delivering 208,795kW (280,000shp) to four shafts

Performance: Maximum speed 30+kts; range 14,805km (9,200mls) at 20kts

Complement: 150+2,645, plus a carrier air-wing complement of about 2,150

Displacement: 72,700 tons light, 81,600 tons standard and 91,485 tons full load (CVNs 68–70) or 96,350 tons full load (CVNs 71–73)

Dimensions: length 332.9m (1,092ft); beam 40.8m (134ft); draught 11.3m (37ft); flight deck width 76.8m (252ft)

Gun Armament: Two 20mm (0.8in) Phalanx Mk 15 close-in weapon system mountings

Missile Armament: Three Mk 29 launchers for 24 RIM-7 Sea Sparrow surface-to-air missiles

Aircraft: 90+

Propulsion: Two pressurized-water cooled nuclear reactors (Westinghouse A4W or General Electric A1G) supplying steam to four sets of geared turbines delivering 193,880kW (260,000shp) to four shafts

Performance: Maximum speed 30+kts

Complement: 3,300, and a carrier air wing strength of 3,000

KIDD CLASS GUIDED MISSILE DESTROYER

OLIVER HAZARD PERRY or FFG 7 CLASS
GUIDED MISSILE FRIGATE

AVENGER CLASS
MINE-COUNTERMEASURES VESSEL

TARAWA CLASS AMPHIBIOUS ASSAULT SHIP

Displacement: 6,210 tons standard and 9,200 tons full load
Dimensions: length 171.6m (563ft); beam 16.8m (55ft); draught 9.1m (30ft) to sonar dome
Gun Armament: Two 127mm (5in) L/54 DP in two Mk 45 single mountings, and two 20mm (0.79in) Phalanx Mk 15 close-in weapon system mountings
Missile Armament: Two quadruple container-launchers for eight RGM-84A Harpoon surface-to-surface missiles, and two Mk 26 twin launchers for 52 RIM-67A Standard-ER surface-to-air missiles
Anti-submarine Armament: Two triple Mk 32 tube mountings for 324mm (12.75in) Mk 46 A/S torpedoes, 16 RUR-5A ASROC missiles (fired from the Mk 26 launchers), and helicopter-launched weapons

Aircraft: Two Kaman SH-2F Seasprite helicopters
Propulsion: Four General Electric LM 2500 gas turbines delivering 59,655kW (80,000shp) to two shafts
Performance: Maximum speed 33kts; range 14,805km at 17kts or 6,115km (3,800mls) at 30kts
Complement: 20+318

Displacement: 3,605 tons full load
Dimensions: length 135.6m (445ft); beam 13.7m (45ft); draught 5.7m (24.5ft) to sonar dome
Gun Armament: One 76mm (3in) L/62 DP OTO-Melara Compact in a Mk 75 single mounting, and one 20mm (0.79in) Phalanx Mk 15 close-in weapon system mounting
Missile Armament: One Mk 13 single launcher for 40 RGM-84A Harpoon surface-to-surface and RIM-66 standard-MR surface-to-air missiles
Anti-submarine Armament: Two triple Mk 32 tube mountings for 324mm (12.75in) Mk 46 A/S torpedoes, and helicopter-launched weapons
Aircraft: Two Kaman SH-2F Seasprite helicopters

Propulsion: Two General Electric LM 2500 gas turbines delivering 30,575kW (41,000shp) to one shaft
Performance: Maximum speed 29kts; range 8,370km (5,200mls) at 20kts
Complement: 11+153, and an air unit strength of 46

Displacement: 1,040 tons full load
Dimensions: length 64.0m (210ft); beam 13.5m (44.3ft); draught 3.2m (10.5ft)
Gun Armament: Two 12.7mm (0.5in) heavy machine-guns
Electronics: One Westinghouse SPS-55 surface-search radar, and SQQ-30 sonar
Propulsion: Four Waukesha diesels delivering power to two shafts
Performance: Maximum speed 14kts
Complement: 5+57

Displacement: 39,300 tons full load
Dimensions: length 249.9m (820ft); beam 32.3m (106ft); draught 7.9m (26ft)
Gun Armament: Three 127mm (5in) L/54 DP in three Mk 45 single mountings, six 20mm (0.79in) AA in six Mk 67 single mountings, and (to be fitted) two 20mm (0.79in) Phalanx Mk 16 close-in weapon system mountings
Missile Armament: Two Mk 25 launchers for RIM-7 Sea Sparrow surface-to-air missiles (to be removed when CIWS is fitted)
Aircraft: Up to 19 Sikorsky CH-53 Sea Stallion or 26 Boeing Vertol Ch-46 Sea Knight helicopters, and (by a reduction in embarked helicopter strength) a small number of BAe/McDonnell Douglas AV-8A Harrier aircraft

Propulsion: Two Combustion Engineering boilers supplying steam to two sets of Westinghouse geared turbines delivering 104,400kW (140,000shp) to two shafts
Performance: Maximum speed 24kts; range 18,505km (11,500mls) at 20kts
Complement: 90+812

Index

Previous pages: 'Los Angeles' class USS *City of Corpus Christi* (SSN 705) nuclear-powered fleet submarine.

Facing page: An aerial stern view of the nuclear-powered attack aircraft carrier USS *Nimitz.*